ENVIRONMENT AND DEVELOPMENT IN MEXICO

Significant Issues Series
Timely books presenting current CSIS research and analysis of interest to the academic, business, government, and policy communities.
Managing editor: Roberta L. Howard

For four decades, the **Center for Strategic and International Studies (CSIS)** has been dedicated to providing world leaders with strategic insights on—and policy solutions to—current and emerging global issues.

CSIS is led by John J. Hamre, formerly deputy secretary of defense, who has been president and CEO since April 2000. It is guided by a board of trustees chaired by former senator Sam Nunn and consisting of prominent individuals from both the public and private sectors.

The CSIS staff of 190 researchers and support staff focus primarily on three subject areas. First, CSIS addresses the full spectrum of new challenges to national and international security. Second, it maintains resident experts on all of the world's major geographical regions. Third, it is committed to helping to develop new methods of governance for the global age; to this end, CSIS has programs on technology and public policy, international trade and finance, and energy.

Headquartered in Washington, D.C., CSIS is private, bipartisan, and tax-exempt. CSIS does not take specific policy positions; accordingly, all views expressed herein should be understood to be solely those of the authors.

The **Yale Center for Environmental Law and Policy (YCELP)** was established in 1994 by the Yale Law School and the Yale School of Forestry and Environmental Studies. The center draws on resources throughout Yale University to develop and advance environmental policy locally, regionally, nationally, and globally. The Sustainable Americas Project was established by the YCELP and the Global Environment and Trade Study (GETS). Since 1998, the project has conducted research and workshops on the links between trade, investment, and environmental issues with a focus on the Americas integration process.

The CSIS Press
Center for Strategic and International Studies
1800 K Street, N.W., Washington, D.C. 20006
Telephone: (202) 887-0200 Fax: (202) 775-3199
E-mail: books@csis.org Web: www.csis.org

ENVIRONMENT AND DEVELOPMENT IN MEXICO

RECOMMENDATIONS FOR RECONCILIATION

JAN GILBREATH

FOREWORD BY JANINE FERRETTI

PUBLISHED IN COOPERATION WITH THE
YALE CENTER FOR ENVIRONMENTAL LAW AND POLICY

THE CSIS PRESS

Center for Strategic
and International Studies
Washington, D.C.

Significant Issues Series, Volume 25, Number 2

Printed on recycled paper in the United States of America
Cover design by Robert L. Wiser

07 06 05 04 03 5 4 3 2 1

ISSN 0736-7136
ISBN 0-89206-423-4

Library of Congress Cataloging-in-Publication Data

Gilbreath, Jan.
Environment and development in Mexico : recommendations for reconciliation / Jan Gilbreath ; foreword by Janine Ferretti.
p. cm. — (Significant issues series, ISSN 0736-7136 ; v. 25, no. 2)
"Published in cooperation with the Yale Center for Environmental Law and Policy."
Includes bibliographical references and index.
ISBN 0-89206-423-4
1. Sustainable development--Mexico. 2. Industrialization—Environmental aspects—Mexico. 3. Environmental policy—Mexico. 4. Environmental protection—Mexico. I. Yale Center for Environmental Law and Policy. II. Title. III. Series.
HC140.E5 R53 2003
333.7'0972--dc21
2002154404

CONTENTS

TABLES

FOREWORD

Janine Ferretti

THE DEEPENING OF TRADE AND INVESTMENT RELATIONSHIPS AMONG countries generally promotes economic growth. One of the key issues in deepening economic integration among countries is how each nation responds to the strains on natural resources that result from accelerated economic growth.

In the case of the North American Free Trade Agreement, both the United States and Mexico have benefited substantially from the deepening trade and investment relationships. The United States' two-way trade with NAFTA partners has been particularly dynamic since 1994—it has nearly doubled, increasing from $333.2 billion in 1994 to $612.6 billion in 2001, which exceeds U.S. trade with Europe and Japan combined. As this trade relationship has grown, the governments of both countries have responded to the environmental challenges posed by deepening economic integration with a broader level of cooperation.

That attention to the need for environmental protection under NAFTA is beginning to have a broader impact as economic integration deepens through the Americas. One conclusion to be drawn from these deepening economic ties is that free-trade arrangements contribute to better economic performance and, if properly tied to

---

JANINE FERRETTI is chief of the Environment Division of the Sustainable Development Department at the Inter-American Development Bank. The views expressed here are hers only and do not represent the views of the IDB.

concerns like natural resource protection, to the achievement of broader social goals.

The research and underlying conclusions of this book show that NAFTA's environmental institutions have been partly responsible for the deepening technical cooperation on environmental protection issues between the United States and Mexico, particularly on issues of transboundary natural resource management. Equally important, the linkages forged under closer economic cooperation have had a beneficial effect on Mexico's ability to analyze and protect its own resources and to identify the linkages between continued economic growth and protection of natural resources. This, in essence, is environmental capacity building.

NAFTA has indirectly influenced Mexico's environmental capacity building by contributing to Mexico's political modernization. Rule of law, transparency in government regulations, broader participation by citizens, and freedom from the state—all are values promoted and reinforced by NAFTA.

The analysis in this book also shows that U.S. technical cooperation with Mexico represents only one aspect of the nation's advances in integrating economic and natural resource protection policies. Mexican civil society, which has gained power as Mexico has opened its economy to trade and investment, is pressuring its own government for better environmental protection policies.

Transferring NAFTA's Environmental Lessons to the Americas

One of the benefits of closer environmental cooperation with Mexico under NAFTA is the demonstration effect on other regions of the Americas. As the United States concludes free trade negotiations with Chile, both parties have committed to enforce their domestic labor and environmental laws, just as Canada, the United States, and Mexico made similar commitments under NAFTA. Cooperative projects under the Chilean-U.S. agreement include efforts to protect wildlife, improve resource management, and reduce the use of dangerous chemicals.

A U.S.-Chilean free trade agreement also demonstrates the United States' commitment to free trade throughout the hemisphere and sets the stage for broader trade liberalization, thus providing additional opportunities to address the environmental well-being of a broader region. In addition to the exchange of goods and services under a trade agreement, the exchange of knowledge and techniques can lead to more efficient production methods and the dissemination of technologies to reduce costs and protect the environment.

Understanding Mexico's Development Path

NAFTA marks only one recent period in the evolution of Mexico's environmental policies, as this book demonstrates. Mexico has been slowly building governmental capacity to manage its natural resources over the past 30 years. These decades also have been marked by phenomenal economic growth, which, in turn, has resulted in higher levels of natural resource depletion. Economic integration with the United States has helped Mexico maintain higher levels of economic growth, but the more rapid growth also strains resources and increases the total volume of industrial activity.

As natural resource strains grow, however, so do the technical assistance programs to resolve them. The most profound regulatory and environmental management changes in Mexican history have occurred in the period from 1988, when Mexico first implemented an omnibus environmental act, to the present, as the federal government attempts to integrate environmental and economic policy goals. This period of rapid environmental transition coincides with the period of economic integration with the United States. In the pre- and post-NAFTA period, the U.S. government, NAFTA institutions, and international organizations all have exercised considerable influence on Mexico's environmental policy.

With the technical assistance and funding provided by other nations and international institutions, the Mexican government substantially reinforced its environmental regulatory regime throughout the 1990s and developed a number of new programs and techniques to assist in defining, quantifying, and addressing the nation's environmental challenges. These efforts have had some concrete results, including the near elimination of air quality emergencies in Mexico City; reduced use of certain toxic chemicals, such as DDT; and an increase over the past decade in the percentage of the Mexican population that has access to potable water and sewerage systems.

Deepening Environmental Challenges

As Mexico's environmental institutions and management techniques have developed, however, the magnitude of the environmental challenges that the nation faces have become more severe. A substantial lag time existed between the first warning signs of environmental deterioration in the 1950s and the development of effective management programs to address and slow the rate of that deterioration. Mexico's current problems with soil erosion, related deforestation, and water contamination and supply pose substantial challenges to the nation's future economic development as well as to the well-being of its population.

Mexican president Vicente Fox has stated that environmental deterioration—primarily a result of water overuse and contamination, deforestation, and soil erosion—is costing Mexico about 11 percent of its gross domestic product annually. By Mexico's own estimates, per capita water supply is expected to continue dropping until 2025. Mexico's groundwater supply, like its surface water supply, also is dwindling. Soil erosion and deforestation are equally serious problems. A total of 64 percent of Mexican territory is affected by some degree of soil erosion; as a result, agricultural fertility is declining. Mexico's environmental ministry reports that most of the erosion is attributable to deforestation. Partly because of soil erosion, about 60 percent of Mexico's territory is seriously affected by desertification, much of which may not be reversible.

Cost of the Environmental Challenges

Insufficient funding is the most significant impediment to solving Mexico's environmental challenges. As this book shows, Mexico faces a series of internal financial decisions in order to deal effectively with its natural resource base. Part of the Mexican government's challenge is the financial cost of periodic domestic financial crises that cause government spending to shrink and then expand, resulting in inconsistent environmental policy development and implementation. This problem arose in the early 1970s, in the 1980s, and again after the 1994 financial crisis.

With each of the deepening environmental challenges since the 1980s, however, industrialized countries and multilateral funding institutions have given varying amounts of technical assistance and funding to help the Mexican government address critical issues of technology, planning, monitoring, and data analysis. The closer relationship between the United States and Mexico under NAFTA has tended to increase this assistance, providing Mexico with another indirect benefit from its deepening economic integration with North America.

The linkages between Mexico's natural resource base and its future economic development are important lessons to keep in mind as economic integration advances throughout the Western Hemisphere. Economic growth is an important component of better living, but only if its advantages can be sustained from one generation to the next.

ACKNOWLEDGMENTS

Jan Gilbreath

THE ANALYSIS IN THIS BOOK HAS BEEN GREATLY STRENGTHENED BY the work of key trade and environmental policy specialists who reviewed it, and I greatly appreciate their efforts. These individuals include the following:

Monica Araya, director, Sustainable Development Project, Yale Center for Environmental Law and Policy;

Christian Avérous, head, Environmental Performance and Information Division, Organization for Economic Cooperation and Development;

Nadim Khouri, senior natural resources management specialist, Unit of Environmentally and Socially Sustainable Development, Latin America and Caribbean Region, World Bank;

Mario J. Molina, professor, Massachusetts Institute of Technology;

Patrick Whelan, Office of International Activities, U.S. Environmental Protection Agency; and

Sidney Weintraub, William E. Simon Chair in Political Economy and director of the Americas Program, Center for Strategic and International Studies (CSIS).

This book is one of two studies on North American environmental policy sponsored jointly by the Mexico Project of the CSIS Americas Program and the Sustainable Americas Project of the Yale Center for Environmental Law and Policy. I appreciate their support in making this project possible. I wish also to thank the William and Flora

Hewlett Foundation for the provision of funds to the CSIS Mexico Project. A special thanks goes to Armand Peschard-Sverdrup, director of the Mexico Project, for his insight into U.S.-Mexican binational politics.

A special tribute also goes to the Mexican governmental and nongovernmental officials interviewed for this project. Their years of experience in shaping and analyzing Mexican policy development enriched my own understanding greatly.

Lastly, neither CSIS nor the Yale Center for Environmental Law and Policy take specific policy positions. Thus, the views and recommendations expressed in this publication are solely my own.

ABBREVIATIONS AND ACRONYMS

BECC	Border Environment Cooperation Commission
CEC	North American Commission for Environmental Cooperation
Concamin	Confederación de Camaras Industriales (Confederation of Industrial Chambers)
DOI	Department of the Interior (U.S.)
Economía	Secretaría de Economía (Ministry of the Economy) (2000 to present)
EPA	Environmental Protection Agency (U.S.)
FTAA	Free Trade Area of the Americas
GDP	gross domestic product
GEF	Global Environment Facility (United Nations)
Haztraks	Hazardous Waste Tracking System
IBEP	Integrated Environmental Plan for the Mexico-U.S. Border Area
INEGI	Instituto Nacional de Estadística, Geografía e Informática (National Institute of Statistics, Geography, and Informatics)
NAAEC	North American Agreement on Environmental Cooperation
NADB	North American Development Bank
NAFTA	North American Free Trade Agreement
OECD	Organization for Economic Cooperation and Development

PCB	polychlorinated biphenyl
Pemex	Petróleos Mexicanos
POP	persistent organic pollutant
Profepa	Procuraduría Federal de Protección al Ambiente (Office of the Federal Attorney General for Environmental Protection)
Pronare	Programa Nacional de Reforestación (National Reforestation Program)
Secofi	Secretaría de Comercio y Fomento Industrial (Ministry of Commerce and Industrial Promotion) (through 2000)
Sedue	Secretaría de Desarrollo Urbano y Ecología (Ministry of Urban Development and Ecology) (1982–1992); changed to Sedesol
Sedesol	Secretaría de Desarrollo Social (Ministry of Social Development) (1992–1994); changed to Semarnap
Semarnap	Secretaría de Medio Ambiente, Recursos Naturales y Pesca (Ministry for Environment, Natural Resources, and Fisheries) (1994–2000); changed to Semarnat
Semarnat	Secretaria de Medio Ambiente y Recursos Naturales (Ministry for Environment and Natural Resources) (2000 to present)
USAID	U.S. Agency for International Development

CHAPTER ONE

MEXICO'S PATH

ALL COUNTRIES FOLLOW SOME TRAJECTORY UNDER WHICH ECONOMIC development begins and the capacity to manage natural resources gradually develops. Generally, management programs develop as environmental stresses become evident. Each country's ability to incorporate environmental policies into economic structures depends on that country's political and economic structures, however. Political instability or periodic financial or fiscal crises will necessarily prolong the lag time. Mexico is one of the most politically stable countries in Latin America, but it is a country that periodically experiences acute financial crises.

The longer the lag time between economic development and the development of environmental institutions, programs, and management principles, the more serious environmental deterioration becomes and the more costly it is to reverse. If a government ignores the need for environmental protection long enough, the resulting depletion of natural resources poses a threat to continued development.

From the 1950s onward, the growth in Mexico's gross domestic product was based on the availability of abundant and inexpensive natural resources, particularly energy resources. These resources allowed Mexico to accelerate its development in sectors like electricity, oil, petrochemicals, steel, and certain types of manufacturing. But these activities also generated pollution and depleted vital natural resources, resulting in significant environmental stresses.

Mexico's experience is common to that of many countries. In 1999, the Organization for Economic Cooperation and Development (OECD) identified lack of institutional capacity as one of the most common bottlenecks in the development process for many low- and middle-income countries. One significant example is the inability of many countries to integrate environmental protection into industrial development policies during periods of rapid economic growth. Often that growth is made possible by liberalization of trade and foreign investment policies before countries establish the legal regime or the institutions needed to deal with the environmental effects of that growth.

The success of deepening economic integration depends in part on understanding the differences and similarities in national policies that promote or inhibit continued economic development and in understanding the differences in the standards set for commercial and government operations. Social policies guiding education, infrastructure development, government operations, urban planning, and use of natural resources are all factors that shape economic development and, ultimately, the level of regional economic integration that is possible.

A growing interest in economic integration in the Americas led to the Summit of the Americas process over the past decade; this process, in turn, generated negotiations for a Free Trade Area of the Americas agreement. In considering the elements of economic integration, summit leaders have consistently called for additional study of environmental issues of common concern to the hemisphere. If hemispheric leaders continue to focus on environmental goals as part of the ongoing process of economic integration, they will discover the following facts:

- The region's 34 governments have varying capacities to implement such goals.
- The relative strengths and weaknesses of each government's environmental policies are largely unknown.
- The stresses on natural resources vary significantly from country to country.

This study details the path that one country—Mexico—has taken to integrate its development and environmental policies during a lengthy process of economic integration with the United States. The analysis tracks the lag time between development of stresses on natural resources in Mexico and the development of the government's capacity to deal with those stresses. Over the past 15 years, Mexico has experienced a profound change in the development of both its environmental institutions and its economy. Many of these changes occurred in the face of rapid economic growth fueled by economic integration with the United States. Thus, understanding what shapes environmental trends in Mexico may reveal the role that economic integration can play in shaping environmental policy in other parts of the hemisphere.

DEFINITION OF ENVIRONMENTAL CAPACITY

For purposes of this study, environmental capacity refers to a society's ability to respond to environmental challenges. The greatest part of that challenge must be met through government programs, and the government's environmental capacity is measured by analyzing the growth in the use of management tools and specific management programs as well as changes in environmental protection goals. The efficiency of government institutions, programs, and practices in protecting environmental quality depends on many factors, the most important of which are the following:

- level of priority that a government places on environmental protection;
- quality of information available about the causes of environmental stress and the rates of environmental deterioration;
- ability to monitor industrial emissions and use of natural resources;
- ability to use environmental data for planning and mitigation purposes;
- knowledge level and technical training of staff;
- existence of a regulatory regime that adequately addresses environmental needs;

- authority to enforce environmental regulations;
- level and consistency of funding to carry out environmental mandates and mitigate environmental damage; and
- level of citizens' participation in governmental decisionmaking, because civil society must provide the underlying political support for integrating environmental protection into development policies.

METHODOLOGY

Scope of the Study

This study presents arguments that North American economic integration has played a beneficial role both in accelerating the development of Mexican environmental policy and in integrating environmental concerns into Mexican economic policy. But this study also argues that, whereas Mexico's environmental management capacity has been increasing, over many decades depletion of natural resources and pollution stemming from unsustainable development practices have left the Mexican government with substantial environmental obstacles to future economic development.

Correlation between Growth and Environmental Effects

The study begins with an analysis of the correlation between Mexico's economic growth and the resource depletion and environmental degradation that resulted. To explain the linkages between environmental challenges and the demand for policy changes, the analysis then shifts to a history of the development of Mexico's environmental policy and a self-assessment of the country's environmental policy. The assessment is based on interviews with representatives of Mexican environmental, trade, and nongovernmental organizations, as well as on written positions by Mexican government and nongovernment officials.

Outside Influences

The third element of this study is an analysis of the effects of both regional economic integration and globalization on the development of Mexico's environmental policy. This part of the analysis characterizes U.S. and trade-related influences on Mexican policy as well as the pressures that other multilateral environmental and economic development institutions exert. The impact on Mexico's environmental policy that resulted from North American economic integration tended to be reinforced over time by the influences of multilateral institutions and other nations outside North America. For this reason these influences are discussed in some detail.

Environmental Management Tools

Each time the Mexican government initiates a response to a crisis involving resource depletion or environmental degradation, the government must surmount significant obstacles. The government's ability to do so is directly related to its capacity to manage. Mexico has made many changes in its environmental programs over the past five years, but questions remain as to how many management tools and techniques the government has been able to adopt effectively in its efforts to deal with these challenges. The analysis of environmental management tools adopted in Mexico, therefore, explores the extent to which the government has been able to effectively adopt the tools and techniques that will be useful not only in dealing with crises but also in reaching the government's stated goals for sustainable development.

Approaches to Surmounting Environmental Challenges

The discussion of Mexico's use of environmental management tools leads to the analyses—presented in chapters 6 and 7—of the way the Mexican government is addressing some specific issues of natural resource depletion and challenges in the handling of municipal, industrial, and toxic wastes. Chapter 7 reviews the government's response to challenges posed both by the depletion of resources and by the accumulation of wastes that tend to pollute existing resources. The discussion includes an evaluation of the level and rate of resource depletion across three environmental media—water, land (including forests), and air—as well as the government's challenges in handling municipal and industrial wastes.

The following criteria are used to evaluate the progress of the Mexican government in dealing with these challenges:

- the ability to gather data and monitor resources and environmental quality;
- the ability to recognize a developing problem and to generate legislative reforms that address the issue;
- the ability to design programs to address the problem;
- the separate ability to implement programs to effectively address the problem; and
- those policy outcomes that can be quantitatively measured.

The study also describes institutional and financial obstacles to implementing the government's goals.

MEASURES OF MANAGEMENT CAPACITY

An environmental task force created by the World Economic Forum identified institutional environmental capacity as one of four components of environmental sustainability.[1] This study measures some of the factors that the task force described as influencing institutional capacity, including (1) scientific and technical capacity, (2) the capacity for policy debate, (3) regulation and management practices, and (4) the ability to monitor environmental conditions.

Governments use three sets of tools to reach their goals of natural resource management and environmental protection. One set is the use of economic instruments—such as environmental taxes, user fees, and systems of granting permits for construction—designed to alter the demand for and supply of pollution by ensuring that the polluter pays the costs of polluting. The second set of tools relies on prevention and includes environmental planning, such preservation activities as establishing protected areas and other ecological buffer zones, and environmental education. A third set of tools involves direct control over activities that can damage the environment—that is, regulation and enforcement of those regulations. Government enforcement generally includes inspections, audits, and civil penalties or fines for violations, as well as the threat of partially or fully shutting down damaging or dangerous activities. In some countries, penalties may be criminal as well as civil.

The effectiveness of all these tools depends on the level of environmental funding, trained management personnel, and environmental consciousness within a given society. The most important factor in raising environmental consciousness is public participation in the planning and implementation of environmental policy. Environmentalists generate the public demand needed to mobilize the government to strengthen its institutions and management programs or to shame polluters into altering their behavior.

A 1999 OECD study on environmental capacity concluded that environmental ministries in developing countries often share certain limitations.[2] These factors also were considered in the analysis of the Mexican government's mastery of environmental management tools. The OECD study concluded that environmental ministries in emerging economies often exhibit the following characteristics:

- They are relatively young, poorly staffed, underfunded, and politically weak.
- They are overly centralized, with limited representation at the local level.
- They have mandates that overlap with those of other ministries, resulting in institutional "turf battles."
- They have limited power to commission, review, and use environmental impact assessments in national planning.
- They are limited in their ability to enforce mitigation measures recommended by the environmental impact assessments.
- They are limited in their ability to enforce existing environmental laws, particularly those based on the principle that the polluter must pay.
- Most of the ministries are ill equipped to systematically assess the environmental costs of development projects before they are approved.

Data Gathering: Interviews and Literature Review

A nation's environmental institutions are most likely to reflect some mixture of the environmental priorities of government officials, industry, and civil society. International opinion also influences these priorities to some degree. In a region undergoing rapid economic integration, a large part of that influence is likely to come from regional trading partners.

This study relied in part on a series of interviews with governmental and nongovernmental officials in Mexico, in the United States, and within the secretariat of the North American Commission for Environmental Cooperation. (A list of the international organizations whose representatives were interviewed is provided in the appendix.) Governmental and nongovernmental officials were identified as the parties who are most influential in shaping environmental policy, although the impact of industry on policy should not be underestimated.

The interviews were designed to obtain experts' opinions on the following issues:

- changes in Mexico's environmental priorities over time;
- changes in the scope and breadth of Mexico's federal environmental programs;
- the possible influence of NAFTA environmental institutions created under the North American Free Trade Agreement (NAFTA) in facilitating that change;
- the growth of joint U.S.-Mexican programs dealing with environmental and natural resource issues; and
- assistance in filling data gaps in the material available on environmental programs and environmental conditions in Mexico.

Most of the literature reviewed for this study comes from Mexican governmental entities charged with protecting the country's environment and natural resources since the 1980s. This review allows for a comparison of changing domestic priorities over time, a Mexican self-assessment of its own environmental conditions and performance, and the government's own perception of the international influences on its environmental policy.

Canada's Role

This study does not stress Canada's influence on Mexico's environmental policy for several reasons. First, although Canadian trade with Mexico is growing, the extent of that trade remains relatively small compared with trade between Canada and the United States and between the United States and Mexico. Second, because Canada does not share a border with Mexico, the number of environmental interactions between those two nations is limited. Third, two of the three environmental institutions created under NAFTA are specifically designed to deal only with U.S.-Mexican transboundary environmental issues. However, it is important to remember that Canada does interact substantially with Mexico on environmental issues through a number of international forums, the most important of which is the North American Commission for Environmental Cooperation.

Notes

[1] World Economic Forum, Global Leaders for Tomorrow Environment Task Force, "Pilot Environmental Sustainability Index," produced in collaboration with the Yale Center for Environmental Law and Policy, Yale University, and the Center for International Earth Science Information Network, Columbia University, Davos, Switzerland, pp. 5–6.

[2] Organization for Economic Cooperation and Development, *Donor Support for Institutional Capacity Development in Environment: Lessons Learned,* Report of the Development Assistance Committee, Working Party on Aid Evaluation, Evaluation, and Aid Effectiveness Series (Paris, 1999).

CHAPTER TWO

MEXICO'S GROWTH AND ITS IMPACT ON THE ENVIRONMENT

DEGRADATION OF THE ENVIRONMENT IS ON THE RISE IN MOST countries that belong to the Organization for Economic Cooperation and Development (OECD), but at a slower rate than increases in these countries' economic growth. The slower rate of environmental degradation reflects many years of evolving techniques to manage growth and new technologies used in pollution prevention and manufacturing. Mexico's growth and degradation patterns do not reflect the OECD trend, however. The OECD measures degradation in terms of the intensity of the pollution, the energy intensity per unit of output, and the rate of use of natural resources. In Mexico, the rate of environmental degradation appears to be faster than growth in the gross domestic product (GDP), although considerable debate exists on methodology and sources of information used to calculate these measurements.[1]

From 1950 to 1999, Mexico's GDP grew at an average annual rate of about 3 percent, and the country's population increased at an average annual rate of about 1.5 percent. By the mid-1970s, the rapid economic growth had resulted in a dramatic increase in emissions related to industrial and energy use. The Mexican environmental secretariat preceding today's Semarnat (*Secretaría de Medio Ambiente y Recursos Naturales*)—known then as Semarnap (*Secretaría de Medio Ambiente, Recursos Naturales y Pesca*)—estimated that, between 1950 and 1970, industrial emissions across all media in Mexico grew by 50 percent; and from 1970 to 1989 by another 25 percent.[2] Using Mexican government figures, the World Bank has estimated that environmental degradation in 1996 equaled 9.43 percent of Mexico's GDP; in 1996, real growth in Mexican GDP was 5.2 percent. However, the World Bank calculated a resource depletion rate separately at 0.89 percent of GDP, a rate that was substantially lower than the degradation rate of 9.43 percent of GDP.

These figures may be understated, however, because they rely on cost accounting undertaken by Mexico's federal information agency, *Instituto Nacional de Estadísticas, Geografía e Informática* (INEGI). In its calculations of environmental cost, INEGI emphasizes the costs associated with air pollution and does not give equal weight to the costs of water quality, soil erosion, and subsequent loss of agricultural production. Semarnap estimated degradation rates by periodically calculating the resource balance for key resources, such as water supply, and by calculating periodic changes in key factors of deterioration, such as total emissions and total amount of soil lost through erosion. (Table 2.1 shows INEGI's calculations of Mexico's natural resource balance for the years 1993 and 1998.) For Mexico, the energy intensity of production is high and rising, lending indirect evidence of a continuing rise in the intensity of emissions. From 1970 to 1990, Mexico's intensity of energy production (the consumption of energy per unit of production) grew by 5.7 percent; whereas for OECD countries as a whole, energy intensity dropped by 35.3 percent during the same period.

Mexico is heavily dependent on petroleum products for its national wealth, and much of the increase in emissions from 1978 to 1982 occurred within the country's petrochemical sector, which is heavily controlled by the state-owned oil and gas firm, *Petróleos Mexicanos* (Pemex). This growth in contamination caused by the public sector mirrors the experiences of other developing countries, where state-owned firms tend to be inefficiently operated, and the inefficiency often translates into higher levels of emissions.

THE EVOLUTION OF REGULATION

In the mid-1970s, about 25 years after Mexico embarked on a program of rapid industrial development and increased energy use to

Table 2.1
Mexico's Natural Resources Balance, 1993 and 1998

Resource	Unit of measurement	1993	1998
Forests	Millions of cubic meters	2,471	2,355
Petroleum	Millions of barrels of proven reserves	65,516	58,683
Water recharge	Millions of cubic meters	8,619	7,430
Water extraction	Millions of cubic meters	11,836	11,984
Water balance (recharge minus extraction)	Millions of cubic meters	-3,217	-4,554
Air pollution (primary emissions)	Thousands of tons	37,238	41,993
Water pollution (principal sources)	Millions of cubic meters polluted	18,015	19,705
Soil erosion	Thousands of tons	548,252	663,644

Source: Instituto Nacional de Estadística, Geografía e Informática, *Estadísticas del Medio Ambiente, México: Informe de la Situación General en Materia de Equilibrio Ecológico y Protección al Ambiente*, vol. 1: *1997–1998*, published in conjunction with Instituto Nacional de Ecología, Secretaría de Medio Ambiente, Recursos Naturales y Pesca (Mexico City, 1999).

sustain that development, domestic discontent over problems with urban pollution became increasingly evident. At first, the criticism came from groups of academic researchers from the principal Mexican universities and from intellectuals. Some of the first nationally recognized environmental groups were formed during this period in response to Mexico City's urban deterioration. The rapid expansion of Mexico City—from a city with a population of more than three million in 1960 to about seven million in 1970—drew public attention to the government's inability to provide basic infrastructure services, and the city's growth substantially raised the cost of providing those services. In addition, Mexico City's air pollution began to have adverse health implications, particularly for children.

Despite the rise in industrial emissions, throughout the 1970s and up to 1983, Mexican environmental law focused primarily on health issues. Mexico's first step toward environmental policymaking was the 1971 Federal Law for the Prevention and Control of Environmental Contamination.[3] Under this law, Mexico established a subsecretariat for environmental improvement under the Ministry of Health. The resulting environmental program was weak and poorly funded, and its primary mission was environmental education. The subsecretariat did generate new regulatory statutes for air and water quality, but these were of limited use, because they were not routinely enforced.

After the 1971 environmental law was implemented, the oil shocks and a debt crisis that sent Mexico's economy into a tailspin stalled the evolution of environmental management. For President José Lopez-Portillo, economic recovery, which was fueled by new petroleum discoveries, became the government's top development priority. By the end of the Lopez-Portillo administration, however, mounting traffic congestion and pollution problems in Mexico City and a massive international outcry over an oil spill in the Gulf of Mexico drew the government's attention to environmental issues. The environment became an official category in national planning documents, and the government began to regulate air quality in Mexico City.

After Miguel de la Madrid assumed the presidency in December 1982, he combined urban affairs and the environment into a single ministry, the Ministry of Urban Development and Ecology *(Secretaría de Desarrollo Urbano y Ecología,* Sedue). Over the next decade, Sedue's operation evolved into four areas: pollution prevention and control, natural resource conservation, standards and regulation, and environmental training and public participation.[4] President de la Madrid also implemented a new environmental law to strengthen environmental legislation on marine pollution, toxic wastes, noise, thermal pollution, and nuclear radiation. In 1983, environmental protection was elevated to the level of a subsecretariat within the Ministry for Urban Development. (Table 2.2 presents a detailed chronology of official steps taken to address environmental concerns.) Before President de la Madrid could reach some of his modest environmental goals, he was confronted with another collapse of the Mexican economy. As a result, the government decreased the amount spent on conservation and prevention and cleanup of pollution.

Nevertheless, a grassroots environmental movement began to raise the issues to the national level, and ultimately, these issues were linked with larger issues of effective democracy and transparency of government operations in Mexico. Environmentalists pushed for a contingency plan to deal with pollution emergencies in Mexico City, a plan for voluntary inspections of vehicular emissions, closure of an open-air landfill in Mexico City, and suspension of construction of a hydroelectric project on the Usumacinta River.

Air pollution problems in Mexico City increased throughout the 1970s, and in 1978 President Lopez-Portillo began an air quality monitoring and regulatory program for Mexico City. The program failed, and the monitoring effort was terminated until 1982.

By 1988, Mexico City's voters ranked environmental issues as a top public concern, just behind economic recovery and personal safety. As a result, the environment had a more prominent role in the election campaign of Carlos Salinas de Gortari. That same year, President Salinas implemented the nation's first omnibus environmental act—the General Law of Ecological Equilibrium and Environmental Protection. The legislation was actually devised by de la Madrid's administration and remains the umbrella legislation under which Mexico promulgates environmental regulation.

The 1988 law defines the areas that are under federal jurisdiction and those that are under state control. The legislation gave the federal government authority (1) to establish environmental standards, (2) to evaluate the environmental impacts of major projects, (3) to carry out environmental protection actions, and (4) to create and manage natural areas that are federally protected. State and local governments were given responsibility for (1) regulating and controlling vehicle emissions, (2) operating systems that monitor air quality,[5] (3) undertaking some limited routine monitoring and enforcement of

Table 2.2
Chronology of Mexico's Environmental Institutions

Year	Event
1981	The Federal Environmental Protection Law is enacted.
1982	The Urban Development and Ecology Secretariat (Sedue) is established.
1983	An environmental undersecretariat is established within Sedue.
1987	Sedue issues a decree on the importation or exportation of hazardous materials or wastes.
1988	The omnibus General Law of Ecological Equilibrium and Environmental Protection is implemented.
1988	The Trade and Commerce Secretariat (Secofi) issues a decree establishing codes and classification of imports subject to sanitary, phytosanitary, and ecological regulation.
1988	Sedue promulgates the first regulation on environmental impact.
1988	Sedue establishes standards for hazardous waste and hazardous waste sites.
1988	Interagency regulations on controlling pesticides, fertilizers, and toxic substances are issued.
1988–89	Sedue establishes a range of environmental technical standards, including criteria for selecting public works sites, such as hydroelectric utility systems; a series of technical standards establishes maximum permissible air and water emission levels for various pollutants.
1990	Five-year National Plan for Environmental Protection defines Mexico's environmental objectives, strategies, and goals.
1990	Sedue publishes first list of high-risk activities.
1991	Mexico's first public hearings on the environment are held in conjunction with the U.S. Environmental Protection Agency.
1992	The National Ecology Institute is created for environmental policy planning and regulation.

(continued)

Table 2.2
(continued)

Year	Event
1992	The Office of the Federal Attorney General for Environmental Protection (Profepa) is created and given responsibility for enforcing regulations.
1992	The Secretariat of Social Development (Sedesol) is created and given powers to develop, manage, and evaluate environmental aspects of policy.
1992	New federal laws are implemented to deal with biodiversity, standardization, and water pollution; water law establishes institutional and planning mechanisms for managing river basins and calls for improvements in water monitoring, modeling, and assessment.
1992	The National Forestry Law is approved.
1992–1994	Implementation of environmental regulatory enforcement regime is implemented; federal inspections of industry intensify and catalytic converters become mandatory for new cars.
1993	Sedesol and more than 350 nongovernmental organizations create a Social Co-Investment Fund to finance nonprofit organizations for community service projects, including those dealing with the environment.
1993	Mexico's electrical industry adopts an environmental protection program.
1994	Mexico's environmental commitments begin under NAFTA.
1994	Mexico's environmental commitments begin under membership in the Organization for Economic Cooperation and Development.
1995	A cabinet-level environmental ministry (Semarnap, now Semarnat) is created.
1995	Mexico adopts a five-year sustainable development plan.
1995	Semarnap announces that the Cozumel reef, one of the world's largest coral reefs, would become a national marine park.
1996	Environmental regulation is expanded to include integrated permitting, new administrative procedures, strengthened enforcement procedures, and enhanced public participation.

Table 2.2
(continued)

Year	Event
1996	The Mexico City area adopts an air quality improvement program with emission reduction targets by the year 2000 of 50 percent for hydrocarbons, 40 percent for nitrous oxides, and 35 percent for particulates.
1996	High-octane unleaded premium gasoline is introduced.
1996	A wildlife conservation program is adopted for rural economic development.
1997	Water pollution standards are revised, replacing industry-specific effluent limits with limits that are the same for all industries, thereby giving greater weight to receiving water conditions.
1997	National air emission limits are set for many vehicles not yet equipped with catalytic converters.
1997	Regulatory reform to the forestry law strengthens linkages between the forestry sector and the environment.
1998	The Mexican Congress approves a constitutional amendment guaranteeing citizens the right to an appropriate environment.
1998	A federal budget line item is created for state and municipal governments to foster decentralization.
1999	Article 115 of the Mexican Constitution is enacted, giving more autonomy to municipal governments for environmental planning and services.
2000	The Federal Sustainable Forestry Law is approved.

Sources: Instituto Nacional de Estadística, Geografía e Informática and Secretaría de Medio Ambiente, Recursos Naturales y Pesca, Estadísticas del Medio Ambiente, México, 1999, Vol. 2 (Mexico City, 1999); and Secretaría de Medio Ambiente, Recursos Naturales y Pesca, La Gestión Ambiental en México, lst edition (Mexico City, October 2000); U.S. Environmental Protection Agency, Office of International Activities, Compendium of EPA Binational and Domestic U.S./ Mexico Activities, EPA 160-B-95-001 (Washington, D.C., June 1995); and Organization for Economic Cooperation and Development, Environmental Performance Reviews, Mexico (Paris, 1998).

regulations and standards for pollution from municipal sewage systems,[6] (4) regulating and disposing of solid wastes, and (5) creating and managing state or municipal protected areas.

With the creation of an omnibus environmental law, Mexico's environmental policy began to evolve more rapidly, as table 2.2 indicates. By 1992, the federal government had published five major regulations under the General Law of Ecological Equilibrium and Environmental Protection in the areas of environmental impact assessment, hazardous wastes (primarily relating to U.S. firms operating in Mexico), prevention and control of mobile source pollution in the Mexico City Metropolitan Area, prevention and control of atmospheric pollution, and marine contamination. Despite legislative advances, however, by 1994 Mexico still had no technical regulations covering environmental impacts, noise pollution, or contamination of municipal wastewater.

In early 1995, the federal environmental agency was elevated to a cabinet-level position within the executive branch and was known as Semarnap. Mexico then made substantial progress in reinforcing its environmental regulations, particularly with the 1996 strengthening of the omnibus act. The implementation of these new regulations continued for two to three years and included, among other provisions, a series of technical regulations for municipal wastewater discharges and technical guidelines for environmental impacts.[7] In 1998, Mexico established a new, more scientifically oriented maximum level for permitted discharge of both airborne and waterborne contaminants and also implemented a constitutional amendment guaranteeing citizens the right to an appropriate environment.

Effects of Oil Production on Environmental Demands

The Mexican government expropriated British and American oil holdings in 1938 and then formed the national, state-owned oil monopoly, Pemex, which rapidly developed Mexico's Gulf of Mexico oil fields during the late 1970s with almost no environmental controls. The resulting marine and freshwater contamination sparked rural discontent in various parts of Mexico. As early as 1979, rural peasants launched a series of protests against Pemex for the large-scale deterioration of marine and land resources, particularly contamination of rivers and estuaries.[8] In response to the protests, President Lopez-

Portillo's administration incorporated programs to address some environmental concerns into the government's National Development Plan of 1978, the National Industrial Plan of 1979, and the Global Development Plan of 1980.

Effects of Urban Emergencies

By the late 1980s, Mexico City's academic and civic groups were loudly criticizing the government's inability to control the city's air pollution. A report generated by the National Autonomous University of Mexico estimated that Mexico City's air pollution had increased by 90 percent between 1976 and 1980. In March 1983, Sedue undertook a series of public forums to inform the public about the government's new emphasis on environmental improvement and to solicit input on environmental issues. Sedue then integrated the results into short-, medium-, and long-term environmental plans.

In early 1987, the de la Madrid administration offered the public a simplistic but well-publicized plan, "100 Necessary Ecological Actions."[9] This became the first of many documents offered to the Mexican public as proof that environmental concerns merited attention. The National Development Plan of 1988–1994—the first attempt to incorporate some environmental concerns into planned development activities—quickly followed that simplistic attempt at publicity.[10]

The year 1992 was a pivotal one for urban strains. That year, accumulated hydrocarbon gases exploded in the city sewer system of Guadalajara, killing more than 200 people and injuring 1,800. At the same time, newspapers in Mexico City were intently focusing on the worsening air pollution in the nation's capital. Of the 795 environmental complaints filed that year with the secretariat with new responsibility for environmental protection (*Secretaría de Desarrollo Social,* Sedesol), the largest category—338 complaints, or 42 percent of the total—dealt with air pollution.[11] On several days that year, the thermal inversions above Mexico City reached a depth of one kilometer, and the ozone concentrations in the city surpassed all known records. Consequently, the government was forced to take public action against industry.

The Salinas administration focused much of the blame on Pemex. President Salinas directed Pemex to begin an environmental protection program aimed at reducing air pollution in densely populated areas and ordered the oil monopoly to begin producing fuels of higher environmental quality. Pemex also was forced to close a Mexico City refinery that had been blamed for substantial air pollution. The federal government also implemented an Industry Verification Program in the Mexico City area, requiring all industries to measure air pollutants once a year.

Backlash from Domestic Industry

Beginning in 1992, the federal government undertook a concerted and well-publicized effort to inspect Mexican and multinational facilities, closing several factories for blatant violations and instituting some modest fines for noncompliance with environmental regulations.

The fines were not large, and the plant closures often involved only partial shutdowns within a given facility—and these lasted fewer than two days. But because Mexican due process for plant closures was minimal, industry was unable to predict when such enforcement might occur, and the unpredictability of federal government actions frightened facility managers.

As Mexico began expanding the scope of its environmental programs, intense political clashes occurred between the government and the industrial sector, which was not accustomed to environmental regulation. The same clashes took place between environmental groups and trade and commerce officials. Ultimately, the industry protests slowed the intensity of the federal government's oversight of industry, except for government monitoring of multinational firms in the northern border region of Mexico.

Semarnap officials complained that domestic industry leaders obtained the support of the Commerce and Industrial Promotion Ministry (*Secretaría de Comercio y Fomento Industrial*, Secofi), in their efforts to resist environmental compliance; these complaints persisted throughout the Salinas and Zedillo administrations. Secofi, now known as the *Secretaria de Economía* (Economic Ministry), is the repository of most of the data gathered on the operations of the industrial sector. Environmental officials complained that Secofi's reluctance to collect or share production and other operational data that might reveal industry pollution levels limited inspectors' ability to monitor industries. Officials stated that these limitations also prohibited Semarnap from initiating a pollution release and transfer registry.

GROWTH OF THE DOMESTIC ENVIRONMENTAL MOVEMENT

Over the decades, Mexico's environmental groups have gained their own institutional capacity. As a result, they have learned to more effectively shape government policy through focused research on issues, linkages with one another and with international groups, and the substantial support of U.S. foundations that fund international environmental advocacy. A component of the change in the Mexican environmental movement's institutional capacity is its use of coalition building in shaping demands for responsible government performance.

As civic and professional organizations became more vocal in their criticism of the federal government's handling of Mexico City's problems in the early to mid-1980s, media attention to environmental issues rose substantially. And as media attention increased, so did the mobilization and proliferation of environmental interest groups. Before 1980, Mexico had few environmental groups outside academic circles, but by 1984, several hundred groups were focusing on environmental issues. In the mid- to late 1980s, much of Mexico's environmental debate still focused on a Mexico City agenda. The most prominent organization was the Group of 100—artists and intellectuals who had a commitment to slow the pace of urban deterioration but had little if any technical training in environmental management and minimal political expertise.

In the late 1980s, the Mexican government began responding to and, at the same time, reinforcing the capacity of environmentalists by sponsoring public forums in which citizens and nongovernmental organizations could air their environmental grievances. Public participation became institutionalized in 1992, when Office of the Federal Attorney General for Environmental Protection (*Procuraduría Federal de Protección al Ambiente,* Profepa) was established, and public denunciations of environmental misdeeds were officially encouraged. By 1994, Profepa had received 9,185 complaints.[12]

By the time Vicente Fox campaigned for the Mexican presidency in 2000, professional environmentalists with substantial training in environmental policy, law, and planning had formed a political coalition, the Group of 25—a network of about 50 environmental organizations headed by Martha Delgado, a spokeswoman for the Union of Environmental Groups of Mexico. The environmental groups had a sophisticated political agenda that found fault with the environmental positions of all three presidential contenders. (The environmental agenda for the 2000 election is presented in table 2.3.)

Over time, nongovernmental organizations' demands for environmental and resource protection have become more sophisticated. These groups now call for specific institutional changes and more targeted goals. For example, the demands of the Group of 25 during the 2000 presidential campaign called for specific environmental budget reforms that would enable the federal government to carry out existing enforcement mandates. The groups also demanded reforms that would force Mexico to improve its integration of environmental policy from the design stage to implementation and enforcement.

Several key Mexican environmentalists are seeking to expand the use of environmental impact assessments, to increase the standardization of environmental regulations and practices at the state level, to improve compliance with federal mandates at the state level, and to enact stronger laws and practices guaranteeing a community's right to know about toxic and other chemical emissions. Environmentalists have complained that, although amendments to the 1988 environmental act did strengthen procedures for assessing environmental impacts by establishing a stronger system for appealing government decisions, the impact assessments are mostly used to

Table 2.3
Environmentalists' Agenda for the 2000 Mexican Presidential Campaign

Topic	Demand
Environmental	▪ Give more budgetary authority to the environmental ministry. ▪ Establish taxes to fund state and municipal government programs. ▪ Increase funding for the section of Profepa responsible for investigating potential violations of environmental law.
Decentralization	▪ Improve planning and coordination among federal, state, and municipal governments. ▪ Delegate more authority to state and local governments. ▪ Establish regional commissions to ensure the efficient use of financial resources.
Institutional	▪ Establish a Council of Sustainable Development that can undertake environmental impact evaluations of government programs and projects related to budget, agriculture, energy, water, transportation, tourism, industry, commerce, agrarian reform, fishing, and public health. ▪ Reorganize federal authority over water treatment and water allocation. ▪ Transfer water pollution enforcement from the National Water Commission to the Office of the Federal Attorney General for Environmental Protection.
Enforcement	▪ Improve coordination of federal, state, and local authorities' efforts. ▪ Improve integration of environmental protection from the policy design stage to enforcement. ▪ Consider establishing changes in the law to reinforce the concept of the polluter-pays principle and provide civil remedies against polluters. ▪ Establish special judicial tribunals to consider environmental cases.
International	▪ Integrate international issues into Mexico's domestic environmental policy.

(continued)

Table 2.3
(continued)

Topic	Demand
Public participation	▪ Create an arena in which the public can better express its concerns on environmental issues. ▪ Solicit broad public input for ecological planning, drafting of norms and regulations, evaluation of environmental impacts of large construction projects. ▪ Establish strong community right-to-know laws and practices. ▪ Create a culture in which environmental information is routinely given to citizens upon request.
Biodiversity	▪ Reinforce and expand the national system of protected land and marine areas. ▪ Reconsider agricultural and animal grazing subsidies that contribute to deforestation so that the environmental costs of production are internalized.
Deforestation	▪ Study the possibility of obtaining international financing for forest conservation programs under mechanisms established by the Kyoto Protocol. ▪ Establish better databases on existing forests by more frequent use of satellite imagery for input into a constantly expanding geographical information system.
Regulatory	▪ Expand the voluntary certification system under which industrial facilities receive Clean Industry certification through environmental audits. ▪ Consolidate and modernize the system of forming technical regulations. ▪ Establish new technical regulations that are based on sound science and address Mexico's most pressing environmental challenges.
Environmental	▪ Promote infrastructure projects for the management of hazardous and hospital wastes, municipal solid waste, wastewater treatment, and the supply of potable water. ▪ Expand and promote the national air quality monitoring network. ▪ Promote renewable energy projects.

Sources: Compiled and translated by the author from data available in Grupo de Reflexión (G-25), *México: Hacia una política ambiental eficaz para el desarrollo sustentable* (Mexico City, April 2000) and from author interviews with nongovernmental organizations, Mexico City, November 2001.

gauge the impacts of federal projects. Environmental groups want more private development projects to undergo mandatory environmental assessments as well.

Environmentalists also complain that a portion of Mexico's environmental law (*ordenamiento ecológico*) has traditionally limited the amount of information made available to the public on proposed development projects. A 1996 revision to the environmental law established a library to house data from environmental permits, licenses, and authorizations issued by Semarnat. Instead of allowing direct access to the materials, however, the law only required the government to compile summaries of its decisions. Interested parties could request information from the ministry in writing, but the request could be denied if a project was considered sensitive.[13]

In 2002, as the Fox administration had promised, the federal government approved the first comprehensive freedom of information law that broadly guarantees Mexicans the right to know what their government is doing. The law will force the release of many new types of information, including information compiled by Semarnat.[14] The new law calls for establishing information units within federal agencies to determine how information is to be released. The law calls for broad release of reports, studies, acts, resolutions, official correspondence, contracts, agreements, internal agency instructions, notes, memorandums, statistics, and even government officials' salaries. As soon as the law became effective in June 2002, Semarnat immediately posted the salaries of top environmental officials on its Web page.

The new Mexican law requires information to be provided regardless of its date of creation and regardless of the format—electronic, written, visual, or auditory. The government entities excluded from the new transparency law are the Office of President, the National Security and Investigation Center, the federal Drug Control Center, the federal police intelligence agency, the federal organized crime unit, and the military.

As environmentalists' demands have become more focused and as public participation in environmental policymaking has increased, the Mexican government's environmental priorities have become more targeted and more sophisticated as well. This is evident in a

Table 2.4
Mexico's Environmental Priorities, 1986

Priority	Action taken in FY 1986–1987
Urban air pollution	▪ Continued building a national air quality monitoring system, primarily focusing on Mexico City. ▪ Expanded the Mexico City Metropolitan Area's air emissions inventory to 500 businesses.
Water pollution	▪ Drafted technical standards for discharges from the paper, sugar, sulfur, vegetable extract, and fertilizer industries.
Garbage collection	▪ Put into operation 12 waste disposal sites in 12 cities and planned the operation of 15 other sites.
Protection of endangered species	▪ Issued decrees expanding the system of national protected areas.

Source: Secretaría de Desarrollo Urbano y Ecología, *Informe de Labores, 1986–1987 (1 de Septiembre de 1986 al 31 de Agosto de 1987)* (Mexico City, 1987).

comparison of the Mexican government's environmental priorities in the 1980s and 1990s with those in 2001, as detailed in tables 2.4, 2.5, and 2.6.

In 1990, after two years of implementing its omnibus environmental law, Mexico was still in the process of consolidating its institutional environmental scheme and determining its environmental priorities and ways to fund them. For example, three of Mexico's key priorities in 1990 involved decentralizing authority to regional governments, establishing an interagency dialogue on the environment within the Mexican government, and conceptualizing a series of ecological planning zones for Mexico. With these goals in mind, the first task was to gather basic monitoring data on the state of Mexico's rivers and streams so that additional rulemaking on effluent limits could be established. The use of economic instruments, like user fees for most municipal services or agricultural water use, was still a vague and distant goal.

Table 2.5
Mexico's Environmental Priorities, 1990

Priority	Description of proposed action
Decentralize decisionmaking authority	▪ Establish hundreds of grassroots organizations to participate in setting environmental priorities. (By 1991, a total of 17 state governments had enacted their own environmental laws.)
Initiate ecological planning and zoning	▪ Devise a strategy whereby industries can be encouraged to move from the largest cities to smaller cities.
	▪ Begin a planning process for urban zoning.
Use economic instruments	▪ Sedue officials discuss implementing the polluter-pays principle in theoretical terms.
Extend system of protected areas	None specified.
Expand water pollution databases	▪ Extend the national water quality monitoring system. ▪ Increase inspection and enforcement of pollution control standards. ▪ Establish stricter effluent standards.
Promote industrial waste disposal	▪ Begin regulation of industrial facility siting near urban areas.
Expand use of planning tools	▪ Form environmental impact guidelines for industrial sectors.
	▪ Consolidate information systems on assessments.
	▪ Create guidelines for prevention and control of environmental damage.

Sources: Ministry of Urban Development and Ecology (Sedue), "Aspects of Mexico's Environmental Policy and the Environmental Situation in Mexico," Mexico City, April 1991; and author's compilation from various other sources.

Table 2.6
Mexico's Environmental Priorities, 2001

Priority	Description of challenge	Potential management actions
Increase water supply	More than half of Mexico's territory has a water deficit. A lack of infrastructure means 10-12 million Mexicans have no water service. The shortage is aggravated by an eight-year drought.	▪ Eliminating certain agricultural subsidies for irrigation and begin charging water user fees ▪ Proposing user fees for various public services as part of the fiscal reform before the Mexican Congress
Reduce water pollution	93 percent of Mexican rivers and streams are polluted. Much of this pollution comes from cities that do not have adequate wastewater systems.	▪ Instituting a system of water and wastewater charges for municipal governments
Reverse deforestation trend	Severe soil erosion from deforestation limits aquifer recharge rates and reduces agricultural land and fertility. Mexico has lost 30 percent of its forests over the past 20-25 years—one of the world's fastest deforestation rates.	▪ Directing the newly created National Forestry Commission to build a funding base for forestry and consensus on use of economic instruments for sustainable practices ▪ Charging tourist user fees for nationally protected lands.
Enhance municipal waste disposal capacity	Mexico has few landfills and little recycling capacity; some municipalities have no wastewater systems. Few rules—and these are only local—govern these services.	▪ Proposing a system of water and wastewater fees for municipal governments as part of fiscal reform legislation before the Mexican Congress
Increase citizen input in planning and decisionmaking	Mexico has broad legislation ensuring access to information and public participation in environmental decisionmaking; but few clear rules were implemented under this law.	▪ Establishing an office within Semarnat to deal with public participation and transparency ▪ Working on more specific rules for access to information
Integrate economic and environmental policies	The environmental minister has called for integrating environmental concerns into energy and agricultural policies.	▪ Planning by Semarnat to integrate environmental concerns in the modernization of the energy-generating sector ▪ Reviewing land practices for tourist developments

Source: Compiled by author from information presented by Mexican Environmental Secretary Victor Lichtinger, presentation to the Mexico Project, CSIS, Washington, D.C., May 18, 2001.

Notes

[1] Marcelo M. Giugale, Olivier Lafourcade, and Vinh H. Nguyen, eds., *Mexico: A Comprehensive Development Agenda for the New Era* (Washington D.C.: International Bank for Reconstruction and Development, World Bank, April 2001), p. 122.

[2] Secretaría de Desarrollo Social, Instituto Nacional de Ecología, *Mexico: Informe de la Situación General en Materia de Equilibrio Ecológico y Protección al Ambiente, 1993–1994* (Mexico City, April 1994), p. 153.

[3] Stephen P. Mumme, "Cleaning the Air: Environmental Reform in Mexico," *Environment* 33, no. 10 (December 1991).

[4] Ministry of Urban Development and Ecology (Secretaría de Desarrollo Urbano y Ecología), "Aspects of Mexico's Environmental Policy and the Environmental Situation in Mexico," Mexico City, April 1991.

[5] The federal government is responsible for setting and enforcing national air quality standards and for maintaining a national information system. It is also responsible for controlling fixed-source pollution and for establishing and operating an air pollution monitoring system in the Federal District.

[6] The *Comisión Nacional de Agua* is primarily responsible for managing water resources and monitoring effluent discharges and agricultural activities.

[7] Ministry of the Environment, Natural Resources and Fisheries (Secretaría de Medio Ambiente, Recursos Naturales y Pesca), *Mexico: Policies to Promote Sustainable Development* (Mexico City, April 2000), p. 234.

[8] Stephen P. Mumme, C. Richard Bath, and Valerie J. Assetto, "Political Development and Environmental Policy in Mexico," *Latin American Research Review* 23, no. 1 (1988).

[9] Secretaría de Desarrollo Urbano y Ecología, *Informe de Labores, 1986–1987 (1 de Septiembre de 1986 al 31 de Agosto de 1987)* (Mexico City, December 1987).

[10] Secretaría de Desarrollo Social, "Protección del Medio Ambiente, Acciones," Mexico City, June 5, 1993, p. 2.

[11] Ibid.

[12] Secretaría de Desarrollo Social, *México: Informe de la Situación General, 1993–1994*, p. 279.

[13] *The Economist*, Intelligence Unit, "Country Commerce: Mexico," London, September 30, 2000; also available at www.nexis.com (October 15, 2000).

[14] "Ley Federal de Transparencia y Acceso a la Información Pública Gubernamental," *Diario Oficial de la Nación*, June 7, 2002, p. 3; also available at www.gobernación.gob.mx (August 15, 2002).

CHAPTER THREE

MEXICO'S SELF-ASSESSMENT

STATUS OF THE ENVIRONMENT IN POLICYMAKING

The administration of President Vicente Fox began the year 2000 with expectations of making substantial progress in the integration of the government's economic and environmental policies. In May 2001, Environmental Minister Victor Lichtinger announced that he was a regular participant in the Fox cabinet's discussions on economic issues. Mr. Lichtinger also reorganized the environmental ministry, set very high standards for transparency in his agency's operations, and included nongovernmental organizations in environmental decisionmaking. Mr. Lichtinger's persistence has resulted in the promulgation of new regulations aimed at providing more environmental information to the public, and, as of August 2001, he had stopped construction of some hotel and condominium developments that had been planned in ecologically sensitive areas.[1]

At the same time, however, the Fox administration, like many Mexican presidential administrations, has discovered firsthand the difficulty of balancing the need for sustained economic growth and protection of the resources that provide that growth. One of the most striking examples is found in the tourism industry. Although the shutdown of proposed tourist sites and other development projects, as instigated by Mr. Lichtinger, was a signal to Mexican society that environmental law would be respected, President Fox continues to encourage large-scale projects to promote tourism. His reason is an economic one. Foreign tourism in Mexico, which has grown steadily over the last 30 years, is one of the top sources of national income. Tourism earns about $9 billion in foreign revenues, rivaling petroleum as a revenue source. Therefore, limitations on tourism are often considered obstacles to eliminating poverty.

At the end of the Zedillo administration, Mexico's nongovernmental and governmental officials evaluated Mexico's current management challenges as well as the evolution of environmental policymaking in Mexico. Part of the self-evaluation came during interviews for the project reported on in this book; some came from statements made by Mexican government officials in interviews with the press. But an equally detailed assessment occurred in a series of public documents that responded in large measure to the first transition in political power in Mexico to occur in seven decades. Much of Mexico's self-assessment mirrors international thinking on Mexico's environmental evolution. In addition, governmental officials within the environmental ministry and nongovernmental organizations within Mexico demonstrated considerable consensus on the environmental issues that merit future policy attention.

In an analysis of its own environmental management conducted in 2000, the *Secretaría de Medio Ambiente, Recursos Naturales y Pesca* (Semarnap) identified four distinct periods in modern Mexican history during which the national philosophy toward natural resources and environmental protection evolved.[2] The first period, 1917–1971, followed the Mexican revolution to the time of intense industrial development. During this period, the goal of managing natural resources was twofold: (1) to exploit resources in order to feed a mostly rural population, and (2) to build large-scale public works projects that would accelerate development. A second period, 1971–1983, was marked by intense industrial development and a growing knowledge that the pollution generated by that development was adversely affecting public health. The third stage, 1983–1994, marked a period during which the federal government made a concerted effort to integrate environmental concerns into development policy, beginning with the implementation of a 1982 pollution law that sought to improve people's health by attacking pollution. The fourth period, from 1995 to the present, has been marked by the federal government's higher-level attention to issues of environmental protection by integrating the policies of various federal secretariats with different levels of responsibility for the management of natural resources.

THE GOVERNMENT'S FUTURE PRIORITIES

At the end of the Zedillo administration, several key Semarnap officials offered a variety of priority actions to help mature Mexico's existing environmental management programs and to make these programs more effective. Rather than additional legislative strengthening or organizational restructuring, these suggestions, made in a series of interviews, focused on efficiency in government operations. Semarnap officials suggested the following measures:

- Increasing the number of modern regional environmental laboratories: Currently, Mexico has only three state-of-the-art environmental laboratories—one in Mexico City and one each in the northern border states of Tamaulipas and Coahuila.
- Expanding the current laboratory system by contracting with and certifying private laboratory facilities to analyze environmental samples.
- Improving training for the auditors and inspectors of the Office of the Federal Attorney General for Environmental Protection (*Procuraduría Federal de Protección al Ambiente,* Profepa), paying them livable wages, and ensuring that each earns certification after training. Several officials complained that because of Profepa inspectors' low salaries, corruption is commonplace and turnover rates are high. Semarnap officials complained that, despite the U.S. government's assistance in training Profepa inspectors, the vast majority of these trainees has moved into higher-paying jobs in the private sector.
- Restructuring environmental functions at both the federal and state level to diminish interagency disputes that inhibit the development of sound environmental management practices. The environmental ministry (renamed *Secretaría de Medio Ambiente y Recursos Naturales*—Semarnat—in December 2000) should

have clear lines of authority to accomplish its goals. The examples cited most often were the disputes between Profepa and the semiautonomous National Water Commission over the monitoring of wastewater discharges and the enforcement of environmental regulations under Mexico's federal permitting system.

- Increasing funding for the federal government's environmental management and regulatory programs. All Semarnap officials interviewed complained that these programs were severely underfunded. They also complained that a disproportionate amount of environmental funding was allocated to the National Water Commission, which, under the Zedillo administration, had received 70 percent of the federal government's environmental budget.
- Using environmental taxes, such as a gasoline surcharge, to provide new sources of revenue for federal, state, and local environmental programs. Mexico had a gasoline surcharge, but it was eliminated in 1998.
- Adding more personnel to management programs. All Semarnap officials complained that, because of budget shortages, all management programs lacked a sufficient number of environmental scientists.
- Increasing U.S. government technical assistance to areas outside Mexico's northern border region. Mexican officials, along with many academic researchers in Mexico, believed it would be beneficial for the U.S. government to consider more capacity building projects in areas outside the northern border region. They believed that a disproportionate share of U.S. funding goes to projects in the six states of the border region: Baja California, Sonora, Chihuahua, Nuevo Leon, Coahuila, and Tamaulipas.

In 2001, the new Fox administration turned its attention to establishing linkages between the deterioration of natural resources and Mexico's ability to continue to develop economically. The new government is also considering the need for new revenue sources to fund environmental programs. The Fox administration's fiscal reforms that were introduced to the Mexican Congress in early 2001 included a number of proposals establishing the use of economic instruments for environmental protection. President Fox considered deforestation one of the top environmental challenges, because the problem adversely affects soil erosion and therefore Mexico's agricultural competitiveness. Deforestation also is linked to Mexico's increasing loss of underground water supplies, which threatens continued economic development in northern Mexico.

Notes

[1] Tim Weiner, "On Tourism, Mexico Now Thinks Green," *New York Times*, August 31, 2001, sec. A, p. 6.

[2] Secretaría de Desarrollo Social, Instituto Nacional de Ecología, *México: Informe de la Situación General en Materia de Equilibrio Ecológico y Protección al Ambiente, 1993–1994* (Mexico City, April 1994), p. 656.

CHAPTER FOUR

DEEPENING ECONOMIC AND ENVIRONMENTAL LINKAGES

THE U.S. INFLUENCES THAT AFFECT MEXICO'S ENVIRONMENTAL management have deepened and broadened in scope at the same time that economic integration between the two countries has intensified. This linkage is evident in the rapid proliferation of environmental and infrastructure accords signed as the two countries integrate economically as well as in the level of technical assistance to Mexico that generally follows the signing of those agreements. Mexico rapidly strengthened and solidified its environmental institutions in the three years after the North American Free Trade Agreement (NAFTA) was implemented and did so at the same time that its environmental obligations proliferated under the agreement's environmental side accord. These changes were reinforced by Mexico's long-standing participation in joint environmental activities and partnerships with the United States in the border region between the two countries.

In general, U.S. influences over the development of Mexico's environmental policy occur along these pathways:

- During environmental crises in Mexico, the U.S. government provides technical assistance for training, monitoring, data modeling, risk assessment, and planning.
- Mexico's environmental management programs grow and adapt to meet obligations of environmental agreements signed with the United States. Some, but not all, of these agreements are outgrowths of economic integration.

- Mexico's environmental management programs grow and adapt to meet trade-related obligations to the United States.
- Mexico's environmental management programs grow and adapt in response to the environmental and natural resource deterioration that accompanies economic development in the U.S.-Mexican border region.
- Over time, Mexico's environmental priorities show some convergence with those of the United States and Canada as a consequence of the work programs implemented by the North American Commission for Environmental Cooperation (CEC). These altered priorities are then reflected in the type of governance and environmental capacity building loans that Mexico obtains from the World Bank and related institutions.
- As U.S. environmental partnerships with Mexico proliferate, so do relationships between nongovernmental organizations in both countries, as well as between nongovernmental organizations and U.S. agencies operating in Mexico. These linkages tend to strengthen Mexican environmentalists' funding, capacity, and political positions in their dealings with the Mexican government.

U.S. influences have had cumulative effects on Mexican environmental policy that work in tandem with domestic pressures for improvement and program expansion. The result of these influences can be seen in Mexico's changing environmental regulations and standards, which show similarities to those in the United States in the areas of air quality, pollution prevention, budgeting, planning, and natural protected area management, as well as in Mexico's plans to establish the use of economic instruments for environmental management.

Nongovernmental organizations also have pushed for additional changes in Mexico's regulatory regime to enable environmental enforcement programs to resemble U.S. programs. For example, Daniel Basurto, a Mexican environmental attorney and member of the CEC's Joint Public Advisory Committee, has advocated a restructuring of the legal authority of Mexico's Office of the Federal Attorney General for Environmental Protection (*Procaduría Federal de*

Protección a Ambiente, Profepa), which would result in stronger criminal prosecutions for environmental crimes. Profepa already assesses administrative fines in a system somewhat similar to the U.S. system.

The discussion that follows details the trends in economic integration between Mexico and the United States. The section also describes the tandem growth of environmental cooperation both as a part of NAFTA and separate from it.

OPENING OF THE MEXICAN ECONOMY

In 1982, after three decades of growth in a highly protected economy, Mexico experienced an economic crisis resulting from the worldwide drop in oil prices and rising interest rates in international financial markets. In response, the Mexican government took strong measures to stabilize the economy and open it to foreign competition. As part of this transformation, Mexico entered the General Agreement on Tariffs and Trade. And in 1987, Mexico liberalized its foreign investment rules, which rapidly accelerated economic ties to the United States. (Table 4.1 summarizes the history of growth patterns in Mexico's gross domestic product.)

As the Mexican economy began to recover from the oil shocks of the early 1980s, the government of President Salinas de Gortari hoped to accelerate the growth by more closely integrating his country's economy with that of the United States. This move, he believed, would attract more foreign direct investment, leading to greater productivity and accelerated growth in exports. In 1990, therefore, President Salinas declared that Mexico was ready for free-trade negotiations with the United States.

BORDER INTEGRATION

Mexico and the United States have a long history of environmental cooperation along their shared border, and over the past several decades, the region's rapid economic development has intensified this cooperation. A 1983 border agreement became the framework for that cooperation, and it expanded with a succession of multiyear

Table 4.1
Mexico's Rate of Economic Growth, 1981–2000
(in percent)

Year	Growth (real GDP)	Year	Growth (real GDP)
1981	8.8%	1991	4.2%
1982	-0.6	1992	3.6
1983	-4.2	1993	2.0
1984	3.6	1994	4.4
1985	2.6	1995	-6.2
1986	-3.8	1996	5.2
1987	1.9	1997	6.7
1988	1.2	1998	4.8
1989	4.2	1999	3.7
1990	5.1	2000	5.5

Source: Marcelo M. Giugale, Olivier Lafourcade, and Vinh H. Nguyen, eds., *Mexico: A Comprehensive Development Agenda for the New Era* (Washington D.C.: International Bank for Reconstruction and Development, World Bank, April 2001), p. 146.

implementing plans, including one in 1992 and a second in 1996. The two countries expect to put into effect a third implementing plan in 2003, and in late 2002 discussions of a draft plan were under way.

As a result, Mexican communities in the northern border region enjoy better urban infrastructure than do communities in other parts of Mexico. However, even this improved infrastructure is considered inadequate for the needs of the population living near the border. On the Mexican side of the border, the population with potable water supplies increased from 88 percent in 1995 to 93 percent in 2000—a much higher supply rate than that found in other regions of the country. The availability of sewage services also increased from

60 percent in 1995 to 75 percent in 2000. In addition, the amount of wastewater treated expanded-from 34 percent of the Mexican border population served in 1995 to 75 percent of those communities in 2000.

The border region has a current population of about 12 million, and the number is expected to double to 24 million by 2020. U.S. assembly plants—*maquiladoras*—operating on the Mexican side of the border account for a substantial part of regional growth as well as for many of the associated environmental problems. In 1990, about 1,700 plants operated under the *maquiladora* program. By 2000, that total had expanded to more than 3,000. This sector is Mexico's most important source of job creation, exports, and foreign-exchange earnings. More than one million people are now employed in the border *maquiladoras*, and the number of workers has been steadily increasing over the past decade.

The rapid growth on the binational border also generated more contamination than governments on either side of the border could manage. Concerns over growing deterioration led to the 1983 signing of the U.S.-Mexico Agreement on Cooperation for the Protection and Improvement of the Border Environment, known as the La Paz agreement. The La Paz agreement applied to only a small number of regional environmental challenges, in large part because Mexico lacked environmental laws and regulations to cover a broader range of issues. One example of that limitation is reflected in Annex 3 of the agreement, which requires assembly plants on the Mexican side of the border to return their wastes to the country of origin—usually the United States. Annex 3 was signed in 1986, primarily because Mexico had neither the regulations nor the facilities to manage such wastes. In 1988, Mexico's implementation of the omnibus environmental act institutionalized the process of sending wastes back to their country of origin. That act also banned importing hazardous waste into Mexico for disposal.

The value of the La Paz agreement was that it provided a framework under which contentious transboundary environmental issues could be negotiated and also institutionalized regular meetings among senior federal officials in both countries. Shortly after the La

Paz agreement was signed, technical working groups of mid-level officials were established to carry out the mandates of five annexes to the agreement. By 1990, however, many local and state governments on the U.S. side of the border, as well as regional environmental groups, began to view the La Paz agreement as too limited to deal with inadequate urban infrastructure in both countries' border region. Environmentalists began demanding a greater level of integration of environmental policy in the area.

The La Paz agreement did not increase U.S. financial resources for use in Mexico or provide new environmental legislation in either country, but cooperation under this agreement led to the first Integrated Environmental Plan for the Mexico-U.S. Border Area (IBEP) in 1992. Today, for example, the funding provided by the U.S. Environmental Protection Agency (EPA) for regional water projects that affect both sides of the border is maintained at annual levels of between \$50 million and \$100 million.

The IBEP's contribution, therefore, was to identify significant environmental problems on each side of the border, to estimate the funding needed to reverse regional environmental deterioration, and to provide a framework under which the two federal governments—in conjunction with state and local governments—could enter into cooperative agreements on specific improvement projects. The major problem areas identified were those relating to poor urban infrastructure—lack of sewage treatment, potable water, and hazardous waste management and disposal facilities. These infrastructure shortages generated most of the pollution on both sides of the border.

The plan, which was renewed and strengthened in 1996, promoted the regional use of a broad variety of management tools aimed at environmental sustainability. Because the border plan's goals are integrated with the goals of two NAFTA institutions—the North American Development Bank (NADB) and the Border Environment Cooperation Commission (BECC)—a substantial portion of the plan incorporates the concept of sustainable development through the construction of environmental infrastructure projects, including new water and wastewater facilities that serve the border region in both countries. But the border plan also supports other programs designed to—

- improve enforcement of and compliance with environmental regulations;
- establish a broad array of consultative mechanisms on specific issues, such as management of hazardous and solid wastes;
- increase the public's access to environmental information;
- provide opportunities for the public to become involved in environmental decisionmaking;
- improve the monitoring of air quality; and
- promote pollution prevention techniques and technologies.

The IBEP was not developed until the NAFTA debate forced public attention onto this region's environmental problems, spotlighted the limited ability of Mexican communities to respond to environmental challenges, and emphasized the potential for worsening problems to occur in other regions of Mexico. The plan was developed at the same time that Mexico was seeking free-trade negotiations with the United States and at a time when public concern over Mexico's environmental performance appeared to threaten those negotiations. One of the three stated goals of the U.S.-Mexican border environmental planning process, known as the Border XXI agreement, is to build the institutional capacity of state and local governments by providing technical assistance, training, funding, and establishment of partnerships that facilitate the flow of information between the two nations. All the goals established require input from citizens on both sides of the border; the process of soliciting this input through public hearings, seminars, and open meetings tends not only to strengthen the capacity of Mexico's nongovernmental organizations but also to establish a culture of public participation.

The binational border planning process also facilitates consultation on various issues that deal with environmental protection, and the process often leads to additional informal agreements—memorandums of understanding and letters of intent, for example—to expand cooperation. As the Mexican government gains experience in these expanded areas of cooperation, officials often take the lessons learned from joint projects with the United States, combine this information with knowledge gained from participation in other international forums, and apply the enhanced knowledge base to environmental management in other parts of the border region and in other regions of the country. Mexican officials also use the acquired knowledge to incorporate new management techniques into the development of a nationwide environmental management system. This has been the case with joint U.S.-Mexican development of environmental indicators for the border region, the establishment of a tracking system for hazardous waste movements, techniques for incorporating pollution prevention into industrial management practices, solid waste management techniques, and monitoring of air quality. Table 4.2 details some of the linkages between border projects and Mexico's efforts to extend the knowledge gained into other areas.

FREE-TRADE PRESSURES

By 1991, domestic and international calls for a shift in Mexico's environmental policies had reached a fevered pitch and threatened to derail trade negotiations. The intensity of the debate generated profound changes in Mexico's environmental institutions, its regulatory regime for environmental protection, and the U.S.-Mexican environmental relationship.

Mexico's interactions with the United States on issues dealing with environmental protection increased substantially at all levels of government in the early 1990s, just as NAFTA was being debated and implemented. (Table 4.3 provides a chronology of agreements among the three North American countries.) These interactions ranged from informal binational meetings to the signing of formal cooperative agreements on a broad range of issues. In summer 1991, the Mexican government—in conjunction with the EPA—held its first public hearings on the environment. Those hearings led to the implementation of a binational border environmental management plan referred to as the Border XXI agreement.

Table 4.2
Mexico's Application of Lessons Learned

Issue	Description
Use of environmental indicators	▪ In 1996, the U.S. and Mexican governments established a working group on environmental information resources. ▪ In 1995, Semarnap signed an interagency agreement with INEGI to establish nationwide indicators of sustainable development, using UN methodologies. ▪ In 1997, the U.S. and Mexican governments jointly published an accounting of environmental indicators for their shared border region. ▪ In 2000, Semarnap published a compilation of national environmental indicators and strategies for incorporating them into environmental planning.
Monitoring and tracking of hazardous waste	▪ In 1986, Mexico entered an agreement with the United States on binational monitoring and tracking of hazardous waste generated by U.S. companies operating in Mexico; the information assisted Mexico in developing a nationwide registry system for hazardous waste. ▪ In 1988, Mexico incorporated provisions of this agreement into its omnibus environmental act. ▪ The Mexican government is now planning a nationwide hazardous waste inventory.
Pollution prevention	▪ To carry out its responsibilities as part of a binational pollution prevention working group, the National Ecology Institute established an Office of Pollution Prevention, which has expanded partnerships among the institute, the EPA, Mexican state governments and industries, and educational institutions on both sides of the border.
Response to environmental emergencies	▪ As part of the border environmental planning process, a binational working group was established to deal with contingency planning and emergency response. Under this program, Mexico and the United States developed contingency plans to deal with hazardous waste emergencies for six binational urban regions.
Air quality	▪ Binational cooperative efforts to monitor and model pollution sources in the Ciudad Juárez, Chihuahua/El Paso, Texas, airshed gave Semarnap expertise in air quality management that allowed the Mexican government to extend efforts to monitor air quality to other binational urban regions.

Source: Compiled and translated by author from various sources.

Table 4.3
Mexico's Environmental Linkages to the United States and Canada

Year	Event or Accord
1936	Convention between the United States and Mexico for the Protection of Migratory Birds and Game Mammals
1941	Convention on Nature Protection and Wildlife Preservation in the Western Hemisphere
1944	Creation of the International Boundary and Water Commission
1964	Beginning of the *maquiladora* program in the U.S.-Mexican border region
1975	U.S.-Mexican memorandum of understanding on wildlife conservation
1980	U.S.-Mexican agreement on ocean pollution from oil spills
1983	Signing of the U.S.-Mexican La Paz border environmental agreement
1983	Sedue and the U.S. Fish and Wildlife Service Agreement on the Conservation of Wildlife
1983	Memorandum of Understanding between Mexico, the United States, and Canada on the protection of migratory waterfowl and their habitats
1986	Mexico's entry into the General Agreement on Tariffs and Trade
1986	U.S.-Mexican signing of Annex 1 (hazardous waste management) of the La Paz agreement
1987	Liberalization of foreign investment rules by Mexico
1988	Memorandum of understanding between Mexico and the United States for the creation of a joint Committee on Wild Plant and Animal Life and Their Habitats and Endangered Species in Mexico and the United States
1989	Establishment of a Tripartite Committee for the Conservation of Wetlands and their Migratory Birds (includes Canada)
1989	Cooperation Agreement for Environmental Protection and Improvement in the Mexico City Metropolitan Area
1990	Agreement to Improve the Quality of Air in Mexico City and its Metropolitan Area.
1990	Beginning of Mexican efforts seeking free-trade negotiations with the United States
1990	Establishment of Mexican-U.S. border environmental working groups
1990	U.S.-Mexican agreement on the treatment and disposal of wastewater for Tijuana
1991	Mexico's cosponsorship of first environmental hearings with the U.S. Environmental Protection Agency

(continued)

Table 4.3
(continued)

Year	Event or Accord
1992	Adoption of U.S.-Mexican Integrated Border Environmental Plan
1992	Adoption of U.S.-Mexican binational Hazardous Waste Tracking System
1993	Signing of a bilateral accord with the United States creating the Border Environment Cooperation Commission and the North American Development Bank
1993	Signing of the North American Agreement for Environmental Cooperation as part of Mexico's NAFTA obligations
1994	Mexico's entry into the Organization for Economic Cooperation and Development
1994	Mexico's entry into the North American Waterfowl Management Plan
1994	U.S.-Mexican Conservation of Wildlife Agreement, under which the two countries undertake 85 projects, including those aimed at increasing Mexico's capacity to manage threatened and endangered species in natural areas and migratory bird habitats and other training in natural resource management
1995	EPA approval of the importation of Mexican hazardous waste to a treatment facility in Port Arthur, Texas
1995	CEC's and other public and private institutions' initiation of an investigation into the causes of an ecological disaster in the Silva reservoir on the Turbio River, in which more than 40,000 birds died; $545 million pesos allocated by Semarnap to clean up the river
1995	Mexico and Canada's announcement of a joint investment of $500,000 to establish an international network of reserves to protect the monarch butterfly
1996	U.S.-Mexican Agreement on Information Sharing on Border Maritime Issues
1996	U.S.-Mexican agreement on a second border environmental plan (Border XXI)
1997	Agreements by Mexico, the United States, and Canada to prepare a binding agreement on transboundary environmental impact assessment to establish common procedures for assessments in border areas, reached under the CEC
1997	Signing of letter of intent by Semarnap and the U.S. Department of the Interior to preserve contiguous natural protected areas and establish pilot projects in the Sonoran and Chihuahuan Deserts.
1999	Announcement by the United States and Mexico of intent to increase cooperation on conservation efforts in the upper San Pedro River basin.

Source: Compiled and translated by author from various sources.

One impact on Mexico's institutional capacity that is strongly linked to the NAFTA environmental debate is a strengthening of the country's environmental enforcement regime. During the NAFTA debate, after U.S. Senator Richard Gephardt expressed his concern about weak environmental regulation in Mexico, the Mexican government energized its environmental program by creating Profepa in 1992. Not only did Profepa conduct hundreds of well-publicized inspections of both domestic and international manufacturing facilities, the environmental attorney general's office also imposed a system of administrative fines somewhat similar to those used in the United States. Profepa also began keeping a running score card of inspections, shutdowns, and penalties in a series of publications written in English and circulated to governmental and nongovernmental officials throughout the United States.

NAFTA

In the three-year period following the implementation of NAFTA in January 1994, the Mexican government made a rapid series of moves to strengthen and solidify its environmental regulatory regime. Based on the U.S. experience, these changes were likely to occur anyway after implementation of first-ever comprehensive national environmental legislation. But the speed with which institutional development occurred in Mexico can be attributed in part to international pressures. The United States implemented its first comprehensive environmental acts beginning in the late 1960s and solidified its environmental regulatory regime over the next 30 years. Mexico implemented its first environmental act in 1988, had a cabinet-level environmental ministry by 1994—a milestone never achieved in the United States—and had a significant regulatory regime by 1996.

Although U.S.-Mexican two-way trade and investment had been increasing for many years, that economic relationship deepened under NAFTA. Total trade flows among the three NAFTA countries increased steadily—from \$480 billion in 1998 to \$619.8 billion in 2000.[1] The United States is currently the destination of more than 80 percent of Mexico's exports. Mexico is the second most important

Table 4.4
Growth in Trade between the United States and Mexico, 1989–2000
(value in thousands of U.S. dollars)

Year	U.S. Imports from Mexico	U.S. Exports to Mexico
1989	$26,556,570	$24,117,255
1990	29,505,962	27,467,595
1991	30,445,131	32,279,218
1992	33,934,561	39,604,899
1993	38,667,664	40,265,478
1994	48,605,259	49,136,046
1995	61,721,000	44,880,776
1996	74,179,119	54,685,865
1997	85,004,793	68,393,219
1998	93,017,358	75,369,300
1999	109,018,159	81,380,740
2000	134,734,402	100,442,094

Note: Import data represent U.S. imports for consumption.
Source: U.S. International Trade Commission Dataweb, www.usitc.gov (April 21 and May 10, 2001).

destination for U.S. exports but ranks third—behind Canada and Japan—as a supplier of U.S. imports. (Table 4.4 shows the steadily increasing value of U.S. imports from and exports to Mexico since 1989.) In terms of foreign direct investment, both the United States and Canada dominate, accounting for 58 percent of the total investment projected for 2000.[2]

The opportunity for deepening U.S. and Canadian environmental relations with Mexico occurred in three ways under NAFTA: by means of the provisions of the agreement itself, the provisions of environmental and infrastructure side accords, and a new emphasis on cooperative efforts between U.S. and Mexican federal agencies outside of the trilateral NAFTA environmental accord. As outlined in table 4.5, the preamble to the agreement and 5 of its 22 chapters address environmental issues, and other NAFTA provisions could have indirect effects on environmental protection.

NAFTA BORDER INSTITUTIONS

When the U.S. and Mexican governments signed NAFTA, they established the Border Environment Cooperation Commission and the North American Development Bank—institutions that serve to deepen and solidify earlier cooperative efforts to improve the environment by providing capacity building assistance to local communities and funding for environmental infrastructure. The establishment of these institutions reflects regional environmental concerns, but it also contributes to another priority of the Mexican government—to find international funding mechanisms to enhance the urban infrastructure needed to continue economic growth in Mexico.

The NADB was established to help finance projects dealing with local water supply, wastewater treatment, and solid waste disposal; the BECC works with local communities to prepare and develop environmental infrastructure projects and then certifies projects for NADB funding. The bank can make loans and give loan guarantees; it also administers the EPA's grant funds through the Border Environmental Infrastructure Fund.

The BECC and NADB have put into motion a mechanism for investing in the infrastructure of the border region, but only with substantial help from a special EPA infrastructure fund. Throughout its existence, the NADB has been hampered by the lack of equity funding available to local communities on the Mexican side of the border. In Mexico, most local governments do not develop, finance, or administer infrastructure projects. Most local communities have no experience with debt financing and are prevented by law from incurring debt in foreign currencies or to foreign institutions. As a result, local

Table 4.5
NAFTA's Environmental Provisions

Part	Description
Preamble	Promises that provisions of the trade agreement will be met in a manner consistent with environmental protection and conservation of natural resources. The signatories also agree to promote principles of sustainable development and to strengthen enforcement of their environmental laws and regulations.
Chapter 1	The parties recognize the legitimacy of incorporating trade measures as enforcement tools in multilateral environmental agreements, as long as the least trade-restrictive measures are chosen as enforcement tools. Article 104 states that the provisions of three environmental agreements should take precedence over NAFTA provisions: the Convention on International Trade in Endangered Species of Wild Fauna and Flora, the Montreal Protocol on Substances That Deplete the Ozone Layer, and the Basel Convention on the Control of Transboundary Movements of Hazardous Wastes and Their Disposal.
Chapter 7	Sanitary and phytosanitary measures allow the parties to adopt or apply measures that are more stringent than those established by international bodies. These measures must be based on scientific principles and should incorporate risk assessments when appropriate.
Chapter 9	In dealing with technical barriers to trade, parties can choose levels of environmental protection considered appropriate to attain national environmental goals, as long as those measures are nondiscriminatory and do not create unnecessary obstacles to trade. Countries must follow the obligations established by the World Trade Organization agreement on technical barriers to trade as well as other agreements, including environmental and conservation agreements. Article 906 encourages countries to make their standards compatible, to the greatest extent possible, without reducing the level of environmental protection.
Chapter 11	This investment chapter contains Article 1114, which states that the parties should not encourage investment by relaxing domestic health, safety, or environmental measures. The article also reinforces each party's right to adopt or enforce measures considered appropriate to ensure that investment is consistent with the environmental principles of that party.
Dispute	A country that complains about an action taken for environmental or health reasons under Article 104, Subchapter 7(b), or Chapter 9, can have that dispute settled under NAFTA procedures.

Source: Governments of Canada, Mexico, United States of America, *North American Free Trade Agreement,* signed December 1992, accessed at NAFTA Secretariat, www.nafta-sec-alena.org/english/index.htm (July 2000).

communities lack the capacity to design or finance major projects to improve their infrastructure.

In response, the U.S. government began earmarking money for environmental projects on both sides of the border. From 1994 through early 2000, the U.S. Congress appropriated to the EPA a total of $575 million for water-related infrastructure grants to be used on both sides of the border. The Border Environmental Infrastructure Fund was established in 1997 to reduce the cost of infrastructure projects for local communities. With this fund, the EPA gives grants for water and wastewater projects in the border region, as long as the infrastructure deficiency affects communities on both sides of the border. If grant funds are used on the Mexican side, Mexico is required to provide an equal investment.

As of March 31, 2001, the NADB had authorized $276 million in financial assistance for 32 projects.[3] Of this amount, $262.14 million in grant assistance was authorized through the EPA's fund. The total value of these 32 projects, including other matching funds, was $870 million. Of these, 25 projects are located in the United States and 19 in Mexico.

Capacity-Building Assistance

BECC and NADB officials quickly determined that the communities on both sides of the border often lack the technical expertise needed to assess their needs, package loan proposals, and implement infrastructure financing schemes for their municipalities. In response, both organizations have implemented technical assistance programs. By March 31, 2001, the BECC's Technical Assistance Program had allocated about $19.9 million to aid in the development of 144 environmental infrastructure projects in 99 communities on both sides of the border. The NADB's Institutional Development Cooperation Program has undertaken 99 projects to assist 65 communities.

Mexico's View of the North American Development Bank

President Fox and members of his administration have expressed an interest in expanding the NADB's activities to other regions of Mexico. Late in the Zedillo administration, some environmental ministry officials also expressed an interest in creating a similar institution that could finance environmental infrastructure projects throughout Latin American under a Free Trade Area of the Americas plan. Although the NADB's geographical region remains limited to either side of the Mexican-U.S. border, the bank has expanded the scope of its activities and available financing mechanisms for infrastructure projects. NADB has met with very limited success in this effort, however.

In November 2000, the NADB's board of directors agreed that the bank could begin financing other projects aimed at reducing pollution, improving the supply of drinking water, or protecting flora and fauna. Funding could also be directed at projects to improve air quality and public transportation and to find techniques to produce energy cleanly and efficiently. Other projects eligible for funding include improving the capacity of local governments to plan, develop, or manage water supplies. Most local governments cannot obtain the bank's loans without supplemental grant funding, however. The grants provided by the EPA, the primary grant funder for NADB projects, are mostly limited to water projects.

The NADB also initiated a Value Lending Program, which can receive up to $50 million from the bank's paid-in capital. This fund is designed to provide loans for water, wastewater, and solid waste projects at interest rates that are lower than those offered by the bank's regular lending program. Another NADB initiative aims to provide needed equity investment for infrastructure projects using undesignated retained earnings to increase private investment in these projects.

TRILATERAL ENVIRONMENTAL AGREEMENT

As part of NAFTA, the North American Agreement on Environmental Cooperation (NAAEC) was signed to encourage greater cooperative measures among the three NAFTA parties. (Table 4.6 lists the NAAEC's major provisions.) However, many officials in Canada and the United States tacitly agreed that the underlying reason for the agreement was to increase Mexico's institutional capacity to deal with

Table 4.6
North American Agreement on Environmental Cooperation Provisions

Part	Description
Part 1	Contains objectives aimed at sustainable development and enhanced institutional capacity, primarily in the area of environmental enforcement.
Part 2	Contains more specific measures aimed at enhancing institutional capacity. The parties agree to issue reports on the state of their environments, promote environmental education, develop environmental technology, undertake environmental research, and assess environmental impacts. The parties are encouraged to use economic instruments to promote environmental goals.
Part 3	Establishes the Commission for Environmental Cooperation, the entity charged with carrying out the agreement's provisions. The commission consists of the parties' environmental ministers and a secretariat and advisory committees serve them.
Part 4	Emphasizes the need for joint cooperation and outlines provisions aimed at ensuring that the parties notify one another of environmental measures taken.
Part 5	Deals with the resolution of environmental disputes. Weak enforcement of environmental laws is considered an unfair form of trade advantage. Thus, if a party fails to enforce its own environmental laws, it can be punished by suspension of some NAFTA benefits (except for Canada, which is not covered by this provision). To date, the trade sanction provisions have not been used.

Source: North American Commission for Environmental Cooperation, "North American Agreement on Environmental Cooperation," *North American Environmental Law and Policy*, official documents (Montreal, 1998).

environmental protection. The NAFTA parties believed that Mexico's enhanced environmental management capacity would help level the competitive playing field during increased economic integration by eliminating any comparative advantage posed by lax enforcement of environmental laws.

The environmental changes that Mexico put into motion during the NAFTA debate were solidified and deepened with the establishment of the North American Commission for Environmental Cooperation. The CEC influences Mexico's environmental institutional capacity in many ways. The most important of these include the following:

- initiating an annual work program that aims to strengthen domestic laws and environmental management programs;
- increasing public participation in environmental decisionmaking in all three countries and undertaking activities that strengthen the culture of citizen participation and transparency of government operations;
- acting as a conduit for the flow of environmental information and technical expertise throughout North America;
- serving as a regional implementing body for environmental mandates coming from the United Nations and other multilateral institutions;
- facilitating funding mechanisms for national governments and nongovernmental organizations;
- offering training to governmental and nongovernmental officials on a wide variety of environmental management issues, including regulatory compliance and enforcement;
- establishing consensus on environmental management goals in all three countries;
- serving as a facilitator for standardized data collection techniques; and
- building on and linking the activities of federal, state, and local governments throughout North America.

The CEC carries out these roles through its work program, research agenda, and dissemination of the results of that research through conferences and symposiums. The CEC is able to achieve its objectives because of its mandate to investigate complaints that any North American government is failing to enforce its own environmental laws.

The CEC's Capacity Building Mission

Building the capacity of government programs to manage pollution and the use of natural resources is one of the CEC's stated objectives and figures prominently in the CEC secretariat's three-year plan. For any given project within the CEC work program, when one of the three parties lacks experience or expertise, the goal of that project becomes the transfer of information or expertise on that issue to the government that needs it. Mexico is often the party in need of information, particularly on issues involving monitoring use of natural resources, assimilating data, using that information for decisionmaking, and disseminating the information to the public.

When Mexico's institutions or management plans limit the country's ability take part in trilateral cooperative efforts, the CEC makes a significant effort to boost Mexico's capacity through the annual work program. For example, because Mexico has not implemented a pollution release and transfer registry, for several years the CEC's program has been involved in preparing both Mexico's environmental ministry and Mexican industries for a first-ever emissions inventory. To achieve this goal, in 2001 the CEC initiated a series of special reports to show how an emissions inventory can be used as a pollution management tool, particularly in setting pollution control priorities and developing new control strategies. Other examples of these activities include the following:

- guidance on undertaking risk assessments;
- techniques for conducting inventories of industrial emissions;
- assistance in gathering baseline data on sources of stress to wetlands, forests, and other ecosystems; and
- assistance in sampling and analyzing substances across air, water, and other environmental media and developing reference guidelines for analyzing those substances in accordance with international standards.

In determining the value of individual work projects, the CEC now weighs each proposal's contribution to environmental capacity building. This CEC effort, evident in its 2000–2002 work plan, has the enthusiastic support of officials in all three NAFTA countries. An independent review of CEC activities undertaken in 1998 also recommended this approach.[4]

One of the CEC's work projects is specifically aimed at enhancing programs designed to build all three NAFTA countries' capacity to prevent pollution. The CEC's secretariat has pushed this goal by organizing roundtable discussions and by initiating a Fund for Pollution Prevention (*Fondo de Prevención de la Contaminación*) to encourage North American industrial associations—such as Mexico's Confederation of Industrial Chambers (*Confederación de Cámaras Industriales*, Concamin) and the Canadian and U.S. business councils—to participate in technical discussions held by committees.

The CEC indirectly addresses issues of environmental enforcement through its capacity building efforts. For example, a part of the CEC's work program concentrates on fostering cooperation among environmental laboratories in North America; the program tends to supplement Mexico's lack of laboratory data analysis. One focus of the CEC's research agenda is to improve the compatibility of environmental technical standards in North America. In addition, the CEC sponsors a project for building capacity to enforce regulations and ensure compliance; the effort provides training for government staff in enforcing wildlife and pollution control.

The CEC's Role in Standardization

The CEC also has begun a process of standardizing management techniques across North America and making those techniques compatible with the goals and principles of environmental mandates promoted by international organizations, such as the United Nations Environment Program and the Organization for Economic Cooperation and Development (OECD). In these efforts, the CEC often reaches beyond federal governments to foster partnerships among environmental organizations, industries, the World Bank, the Global Environment Facility, and individual Canadian or U.S. government agencies. This approach works to the advantage of not just Mexico but of all three countries.

When the three federal governments feel invested in the goals of a specific program, often they are able to promise their own governments' resources to advance the group's goals. Thus, on a project promoting cooperative efforts on transboundary ecoregions, for example, the U.S. Geological Survey may contribute a series of satellite images that help define the baseline data needed to establish trends in the deterioration of a region's natural resources. As another example, on a project to monitor air quality, the Canadian government may provide a mobile laboratory to the *Secretaría de Medio Ambiente y Recursos Naturales* (Semarnat) for demonstration use in Mexico City.

Environmental Information

The CEC's secretariat is becoming a North American repository of information on the state of the environment, thereby assisting Mexico in building its capacity in environmental monitoring and data analysis. In addition to publishing the *Taking Stock* report and establishing or linking existing databases on biodiversity, at its June 2001 meeting the CEC's council agreed to undertake new initiatives aimed at supporting the Mexican government's effort to seek legislation establishing a mandatory reporting system for pollutant releases and transfers. The CEC's support will take the form of building Mexico's capacity to undertake such a system. In addition, the council decided to take the core set of environmental indicators established by the OECD and incorporate them into CEC's periodic reports on the state of the environment in North America.[5]

MEXICO'S VIEW OF THE NORTH AMERICAN COMMISSION FOR ENVIRONMENTAL COOPERATION

In a series of interviews conducted in late 2000, Mexico's environmental ministry officials pointed to five CEC project areas from which the Mexican government had benefited:

- identifying consumer demand and markets for "green" products that can be produced in Mexico for export with minimal environmental costs;

- enhancing Mexico's ability to conserve threatened or endangered species;
- strengthening public participation in environmental decision-making;
- strengthening Mexico's institutional capacity to manage toxic chemicals; and
- establishing an environmental technology fund for small- and medium-sized industries in Mexico.

The CEC has a series of specific work projects and other initiatives mandated by the trilateral environmental accord that fall within these five categories. In an April 2000 publication on environmental policy, environmental ministry officials listed some that they consider to be the most successful:[6]

- establishment of ecoregions in North America and implementation of conservation strategies for those regions;
- creation of a Pollutant Emission and Transfer Registry;
- development of action plans to reduce or eliminate emissions from and use of toxic chemicals, such as chlordane, mercury, DDT, dioxins, polychlorinated biphenyls, furons, and hexachlorobenzene;
- development of pilot projects for sustainable tourism and sustainable commerce in wildlife species;
- coordination of programs for shade-grown coffee;
- studies of the long-range transport of contaminants;
- cooperative efforts on the protection of marine ecosystems, such as the program on conservation of the Californias Basin;
- creation and development of the Pollution Prevention Fund for small- and medium-sized industries in Mexico, in coordination with groups from Mexico's public and private sector;
- experience in dealing with the citizen submissions process, under which complaints are filed alleging government failure to enforce Mexican environmental law; and
- analysis of North American regional environmental trends.

U.S.-MEXICAN GOVERNMENT-TO-GOVERNMENT PROGRAMS

U.S. government agencies enter into many informal agreements with their Mexican counterparts outside the NAFTA relationship. The number of these informal agreements grew rapidly during the NAFTA debate and during the first years of NAFTA implementation. (As an example, see the descriptions provided in table 4.7.) Although informal, these cooperative efforts often enhance the Mexican government's environmental management capacity in the following ways:

- information exchange, including sharing information on best practices for ecosystem planning, mitigation techniques for environmental deterioration, and ways to conduct impact assessments;
- joint research on the health and stress factors causing the deterioration of ecosystems—projects that often encourage both Mexico and the United States to establish and augment new baseline data on water quality and quantity, in-stream flows, water demands, fish and wildlife status, wetlands health, and indicators of air quality;
- technical assistance in the form of personnel training in water management, contingency planning for accidental release of hazardous substances, and environmental assessment scoping techniques; and
- increased public participation in the form of advice and technical assistance on planning and implementing outreach programs to the public.

The U.S. Agency for International Development (USAID) began a targeted environmental initiative with Mexico in 1992. In conjunction with environmental organizations and universities in the United States, USAID provides technical assistance to Mexican environmental groups, community groups, universities, and government agencies. Together, these groups have taken on numerous conservation projects in Mexico, including the Parks-in-Peril program, which is designed to help Mexico extend and better manage its National

Table 4.7
Agreements between Mexico and the U.S. Department of the Interior, 1994–2000

Year	Description of Agreement
1994	The Department of the Interior's nine bureaus establish a U.S.-Mexico Border Field Coordinating Committee to promote, facilitate, and enhance coordination with Mexico on border issues.
1995–2000	"Wildlife Without Borders" program is established; it supports more than 100 projects in Mexico and has resulted in the training of nearly 6,000 Mexicans in conservation and management of the ecosystem and biodiversity.
1996	The U.S. Geological Survey and INEGI begin a multiyear project to coordinate aerial photography and mapping along the border.
1997	DOI and Semarnap sign a letter of intent to enhance cooperation in adjacent protected areas; the effort aims to enhance the exchange of scientific and technical knowledge on natural resource management techniques.
1999	DOI and Semarnap sign three joint declarations to enhance binational cooperation on the transboundary watersheds of the Upper San Pedro River Basin, the Colorado River Delta, and the Rio Grande.
1999	The U.S. Departments of the Interior and Agriculture and Semarnap enter a joint agreement to respond to wild fires.
2000	DOI and Semarnap sign an agreement on cooperation for natural resource and watershed management, scientific exchange, and biodiversity conservation.

Sources: Compiled by author from data available in U.S. Environmental Protection Agency, Office of International Activities, "U.S.-Mexico Border XXI Program, 1997–1998: Implementation Plans and 1996 Accomplishments Report, EPA Report no. 160-R-98-001," Washington, D.C., 1998; U.S. EPA, Office of International Activities, "Compendium of EPA Binational and Domestic U.S./Mexico Activities," EPA Report no. 160-B-95-001, Washington, D.C., June 1995; U.S. Department of the Interior, U.S. Fish and Wildlife Service, "U.S. Fish and Wildlife Service Cooperative Programs with Mexico, 1992–1993," Washington, D.C., 1994; Instituto Nacional de Estadística, Geografía e Informática, *Estadísticas del Medio Ambiente, México: Informe de la Situación General en Materia de Equilibro Ecológico y Protección al Ambiente*, vol. 2: *1999*, published in conjunction with Instituto Nacional de Ecologia, Secretaría de Medio Ambiente, Recursos Naturales y Pesca (Semarnap) (Mexico City, 2000); Semarnap, *La Gestión Ambiental en México* (Mexico City, October 2000); Semarnap, Instituto Nacional de Ecologia, Sistema Nacional de Información Ambiental, "Cooperacion Internacional," www.semarnat.gob.mx (June 18, 2001); and U.S. Department of the Interior, U.S. Fish and Wildlife Service, Office of International Affairs, *Wildlife Without Borders, Mexico* (Washington, D.C., 2000).

Protected Areas system; the Turtle Excluder Device Technology project for the protection of marine turtles; the Ecosolar/Maunte project, which promotes alternative technologies, ecotourism, and watershed management; the Coastal Resources Management project, which creates marine biosphere fishing reserves; an environmental pollution prevention program; an energy efficiency project; and a renewable energy project. As part of its ongoing environmental initiative in Mexico, USAID also was instrumental in establishing a conservation fund that is now used as a model for national environmental funding throughout Latin America. The fund was established with $20 million in USAID money and $16.5 million from the World Bank and the UN's Global Environment Facility.

The U.S. Department of the Interior (DOI) has interacted with Mexico on conservation issues for many decades, because the department's nine bureaus and agencies manage more than 30 percent of the land along the U.S. side of the border. Thus, DOI agencies work with their Mexican counterparts under various international agreements in the areas of conserving endangered species, migratory birds, protected parks, wetlands, and water resources.[7] As in the case of USAID, the level of cooperation increased substantially at the time that NAFTA was negotiated, as reflected in the number of declarations, memorandums of understanding, and letters of intent signed by the Department of the Interior or its agencies and bureaus throughout the 1990s. Some of these key agreements are detailed in table 4.7.[8]

On August 11, 1994, DOI's nine bureaus established a U.S.-Mexico Border Field Coordinating Committee to promote, facilitate, and enhance communication and coordination with Mexico on border issues. The committee received $2.2 million in fiscal year 1996 for its activities, which included work done by the U.S. Fish and Wildlife Service, the U.S. Geological Survey, the Bureau of Reclamation, and the Bureau of Land Management. The 1994 agreement enhanced and deepened ongoing cooperation in a number of areas, an important one being the agreement between the U.S. Geological Survey and the Mexican National Institute of Statistics, Geography, and Informatics, which accelerated the development of digital mapping programs—

first in the border region, then in other areas of Mexico—an essential element in establishing baseline data on the state of the environment by region and by media (air, water, and land).

One of DOI's agencies, the U.S. Fish and Wildlife Service, has substantial interaction with Mexico on issues dealing with endangered wildlife, endangered plants, migratory birds, and training. These programs, which aim to train Mexican personnel in plant and animal conservation practices, have been in operation for many years, with interest having accelerated after Mexico became a signatory to the Convention on International Trade of Endangered Species in 1991.[9] In all, the two governments sponsored more than 70 projects in 1992–1993 alone, for which the U.S. government contributed at least $1 million. By 1996, the total number of projects had jumped to 188, with a total funding level of $4.3 million. The number included 41 projects started under a new NAFTA initiative that addresses environmental concerns associated with increased economic development activities related to NAFTA trade and investment.

In the mid-1990s, the U.S. Fish and Wildlife Service and Mexico's environmental ministry restructured an existing border wildlife program (called Borderlands) into a new program, now called Wildlife Without Borders—Mexico. After Mexico's environmental ministry officials identified lack of trained personnel as a major obstacle to implementing local conservation projects, the U.S. Fish and Wildlife Service included a large capacity building component in its program. From 1995 through 1999, the service sponsored 107 projects in Mexico under the Wildlife Without Borders program, assisted by a series of grants and much larger matching funds from various organizations, for a total of $9,214,025. Of these projects, 41 percent focused on local capacity building, 39 percent on ecosystem management, and 20 percent on information exchanges.

SUMMARY: IMPACT OF INTEGRATION

The speed of Mexico's environmental institutional development can be attributed in part to international pressures, including the pressure brought about by North American economic integration. NAFTA created new environmental institutions in which Mexico is an active participant, and the CEC and the BECC are committed to capacity building projects designed to ensure sustainable development.

In addition, North American economic integration creates synergies under which Mexico's environmental programs benefit. For example, the implementation of the BECC and NADB generated billions of dollars in EPA grants earmarked for capacity building projects for both U.S. and Mexican border cities. U.S. government agencies also enter into many informal agreements with their Mexican counterparts outside the NAFTA relationship, and the number of these informal agreements grew rapidly during both the NAFTA debate and the first years of NAFTA implementation. The CEC also influences Mexico's environmental institutional capacity in many ways.

Notes

[1] U.S. International Trade Commission, *The Year in Trade 2000, Operation of the Trade Agreements Program*, 52nd Report, USITC Publication 3428 (Washington, D.C., June 2001), p. 3-2.

[2] *The Economist*, Intelligence Unit, "Regulatory/Market Alerts—Mexico," London, September 30, 2000, p. 1; also available at www.nexis.com (October 15, 2002).

[3] North American Development Bank, "Joint Status Report," published jointly with the Border Environment Cooperation Commission, San Antonio, Texas, March 31, 2001; available at www.nadb.org (June 13, 2001).

[4] León Bendesky, Barbara Bramble, and Stephen Own (Independent Review Committee), "Four-Year Review of the North American Agreement on Environmental Cooperation: Report of the Independent Review Committee," North American Commission for Environmental Cooperation, Montreal, June 1998.

[5] North American Commission for Environmental Cooperation, "CEC Council Communiqué," press release, Guadalajara, Mexico, June 29, 2001, available at www.cec.org (July 18, 2001).

[6] Ministry of the Environment, Natural Resources and Fisheries (Secretaría de Medio Ambiente, Recursos Naturales y Pesca), *Mexico: Policies to Promote Sustainable Development* (Mexico City, April 2000).

[7] U.S. Department of the Interior, "Criteria and Guidelines for Evaluating Projects and U.S.-Mexico Border Activities," Report prepared for the Border Environment Cooperation Commission, Washington, D.C., April 1995.

[8] U.S. Department of the Interior, "U.S.-Mexico Cooperation on Natural Resources Management and Biodiversity Conservation Accomplishments Under the Babbitt/Carabias Administrations," Fact sheet, Washington, D.C., September 7, 2000.

[9] U.S. Department of the Interior, Fish and Wildlife Service, "Sixty Years of Cooperation Between the United States and Mexico in Biodiversity Conservation (1936–1996)," published jointly with the Secretaría de Medio Ambiente, Recursos Naturales y Pesca, Mexico City and Washington, D.C., 1997.

CHAPTER FIVE

THE INFLUENCE OF GLOBALIZATION

DOMESTIC ENVIRONMENTAL DEMANDS IN MEXICO INCREASINGLY are reinforced in the international arena. As table 5.1 shows, Mexico's environmental commitments began modestly in the 1970s but proliferated throughout the 1990s. International agreements provide the framework under which Mexico reduces industrial emissions, improves data inventory and reporting techniques, sets other environmental management goals, and receives technical expertise to help achieve those goals.

THE UNITED NATIONS

Mexico implemented its first pollution prevention law in 1971, just a year before international momentum for environmental change resulted in the United Nations' 1972 Stockholm Conference on Environment and Development. President Luis Echeverría hosted a preparatory session in Mexico City for the Stockholm conference.

Mexico has been a party to the United Nations (UN) Framework Convention on Climate Change as a non-Annex 1 country since 1993 and ratified the Kyoto Protocol in 2000. The Mexican government has taken several actions on climate change since joining the convention. In 1998, the environmental ministry (*Secretaría de Medio Ambiente, Recursos Naturales y Pesca,* Semarnap) set up an intersectoral committee on climate change and, in 1999, submitted a national action plan on climate change to the Mexican people for public comment.

Table 5.1
Mexico's Participation in International Environmental Accords, 1962–2000

Year of Signing	International Event or Accord
1962	International Convention for the Prevention of Hydrocarbon Contamination in Ocean Water
1966	Convention on the Conservation of Fish and Living Resources of the High Seas
1975	London Convention on the Prevention of Sea Contamination from Shipping Wastes and Other Materials
1976	International Convention on Phytosanitary Protection
1983	United Nations Convention on Sea Rights
1983	Convention for the Protection and Development of Marine Media in the Grand Caribbean Region
1983	Cooperation Protocol to Combat Hydrocarbon Spills in the Grand Caribbean Region
1987	Convention Between Mexico and Guatemala on the Protection and Improvement of the Frontier Zone Environment
1987	Vienna Convention for the Protection of the Ozone Layer
1987	Montreal Protocol to the Vienna Convention
1990	Protocol Relative to the Protected Flora and Fauna Areas of the Convention for the Protection and Development of Marine Media in the Grand Caribbean Region
1991	General Accord for Cooperation Among the Governments of Costa Rica, El Salvador, Guatemala, Honduras, Nicaragua, and Mexico
1991	Agreement on Environmental Cooperation Between Sedue and the Central American Commission for Environment and Development
1991	Convention on the International Commerce of Threatened and Endangered Species
1991	Four-year agreement between Mexico and Japan on technical cooperation on air quality efforts covering Mexico City and its suburbs
1992	Participation in the UN Conference on Environment and Development in Rio de Janeiro
1992	Signing of the Framework Convention on Climate Change
1992	Signing of the Convention on Biological Diversity
1992	Ratification of the Framework Convention on Climate Change
1992	Agreement on International Issues Between Canada and Sedue
1992	International Convention for the Prevention of Pollution from Ships
1992	Basel Convention on Transboundary Movement of Hazardous Waste
1992	Ramsar Convention on Important International Wetlands, Especially the Habitats of Aquatic Birds

(continued)

Table 5.1
(continued)

Year of Signing	International Event or Accord
1992	Agreement to Create the Inter-American Institute for the Investigation of Global Climate
1992	Finance Convention Between the European Economic Community and the Mexican National Ecology Institute
1992	Convention Between Mexico and Guatemala for the Devolution of Wood, Flora, Fauna, and Other Resources of Cultural Patrimony
1992	Climate Change Convention
1992	Convention on Biological Diversity
1993	Mexico-Great Britain air quality agreement for the Tula-Vito-Apasco industrial corridor
1994	Declaration of the Mexican government accepting its environmental obligations as a member of the OECD
1994	Convention for Scientific and Technical Collaboration between the Science and Technology Secretariat of Argentina and the National Ecology Institute of Mexico
1994	Launch of joint activities with Belize on urban development, water resources, and environmental impact assessment
1995	Agreement between Secofi and the UN Environment Program to establish the Mexican Cleaner Production Center to carry out eco-efficiency programs with Mexican industry.
1995	Launch of the Environmental Protection and Industrial Competitiveness Program by Secofi, Semarnap, and the UN Environment Program
1995	Agreement for environmental cooperation between Mexico and Brazil
1995	Complementary Accord on Environmental Issues to the Basic Convention on Technical and Scientific Cooperation Between Mexico and Chile
1996	Memorandum of Understanding on Environmental Protection and Natural Resource Cooperation Between Semarnap and Cuba's Ministry of Science, Technology, and Environment
1996	Program for Sustainable Development for the Frontier Populations of Mexico and Guatemala
1996	Agreement for Environmental Cooperation Between Mexico and Argentina
1996	Desertification Convention
1997	Declaration of Tulum on the Meso-American Reef System
2000	Kyoto Protocol to the Climate Change Convention

Source: Compiled by author from data in Secretaria de Medio Ambiente, Recursos Naturales y Pesca, "Tratados e Instrumentos Globales Internacionales en los que México es Signatario," Mexico City, 2000, www.semarnap.gob.mx (June 17, 2001).

Mexico's international environmental commitments have proliferated since the signing of the Rio Declaration in 1992. Most Mexican government officials interviewed agreed that these commitments, in turn, have placed enormous pressure on Mexican institutions to augment management capacity, particularly in the areas of data collection, analysis, and planning. As a result, Mexican officials have attached greater value to acquiring environmental information and training to enhance their ability to fulfill obligations and to address their own national priorities. The government often turns to international institutions both for funding to carry out these obligations and for technical expertise in implementing plans. These efforts serve domestic needs as well as international goals.

One key example is Mexico's commitment to reduce greenhouse gas emissions. Mexico signed the UN Convention on Climate Change in 1992 and afterward undertook a national inventory of greenhouse gas emissions, modeled future emissions under different growth scenarios, and conducted environmental assessments of the nation's vulnerability to climate change. All these activities gave Mexico's environmental ministry additional experience in data gathering, analysis, and planning.

Another example is the technical assistance Mexico receives from the Global Environment Facility (GEF), which is jointly implemented by the United Nations and the World Bank. The GEF is now providing Mexico with assistance in forming a national biodiversity strategy and action plan and enhancing the country's capacity for sustainable development in six priority regions. The GEF is also funding a Mexican study of greenhouse gas emissions in central Mexico and is helping to implement a related management information system on greenhouse gases.[1]

In February 2000, the United Nations Environment Program and the UN Conference on Trade and Development launched a new capacity building task force that will assist developing countries in integrating their policies on trade, environment, and development so that they are mutually supportive of sustainable development. The task force will focus on building capacity at the national level by using networks of experts and national research institutions. The

United Nations said it was initiating the task force at the specific request of countries whose economies were in transition—countries that have recently given priority to understanding the impact of environmental policies on both trade and development. The task force also aims to help transitional economies participate more effectively in international environmental deliberations.

Another global influence on Mexico's environmental program has been the implementation of the United Nations Environment Program's Clean Production initiative in the early 1990s—an initiative now reinforced by the North American Commission for Environmental Cooperation's (CEC) sound chemical management program for North America. The Mexican government volunteered to become one of six countries that initially piloted the program, and the initiative resulted in an ongoing Clean Production program in Mexico that undertakes an increasing number of audits and other efforts with the country's largest industries.

Various other UN programs dealing with the environment and development have had a lasting impact on Mexico's institutional capacity building. Through these programs Mexico is forced to gather data on a range of issues and to implement action plans to meet certain targeted management goals or emissions reduction targets. In addition to the UN Environment Program, Mexico actively participates in activities and initiatives of the Sustainable Development Commission, the Commission on Trade and Development, the Development Program, the Organization for Industrial Development, and the World Meteorological Organization. Mexico has actively participated in other UN agreements with concrete, targeted goals, including the Convention on Biological Diversity, the Convention to Combat Desertification, the Montreal Protocol on Ozone Depleting Substances, the Convention on International Trade of Endangered Species (commonly referred to as CITES), and the Framework Convention on Climate Change.

Mexico's international commitments intensified within the country when it became one of the first countries to sign the Climate Change Convention at the UN's Rio de Janeiro conference in 1992. Signing the agreement marked the beginning of new obligations for

Mexico to use energy more efficiently, to reduce deforestation, and to carry out new emissions studies in order to implement plans to reduce greenhouse gas emissions, including carbon dioxide, methane, chlorofluorocarbons, and nitrous oxides. Mexico immediately began on an intensive program of reforestation, planting 100 million trees during the Salinas administration. The Ministry of Social Development (*Secretaría de Desarrollo Social,* Sedesol) also signed an agreement with Mexico's Federal Electricity Commission, whereby the company would assume some of the responsibility for reforestation, and began cooperating with the U.S. government on studies to address climate change.

ORGANIZATION FOR ECONOMIC COOPERATION AND DEVELOPMENT

When Mexico joined the Organization for Economic Cooperation and Development (OECD) in 1994, the government took on a number of environmental obligations to better monitor, assess, and provide information on key indicators of environmental well-being and rates of natural resource use. Some of the information required was in areas like sound chemical management—areas that previously had not been priorities in Mexico's environmental management activities. Hazardous waste management, in particular, dominated a part of the environmental agreement that Mexico signed with the OECD. New guidelines governing citizen participation in environmental decisionmaking also became part of the package.

The OECD reviewed Mexico's environmental information system in 1996 and followed up on its review through a series of conferences with Mexican officials. The OECD published an environmental review of Mexico in February 1998 as part of its Environmental Performance Review Program, which analyzes each member country's ability to meet its domestic environmental objectives and international commitments. In the reviews, the OECD evaluates the country's progress in reducing the pollution burden, improving natural resource management, integrating environmental and economic policies, and strengthening international cooperation.

The OECD review of Mexico ended with 54 recommendations of ways that Mexico could improve its environmental performance. In 1999, the Mexican government responded by reporting on its progress in implementing those recommendations. A second OECD review of the environmental performance of Mexico is scheduled for 2002–2003.

OTHER NATIONS

Individual countries other than the United States also have contributed substantially to capacity building in Mexico, particularly on projects dealing with air quality. For example, Japan signed a four-year air quality agreement with Mexico in 1991. Financed jointly by the Japanese Export-Import Bank and Mexico's *Nacional Financiera*, this program provided resources for legislative changes designed to improve air quality, an effort designed to enhance Mexico's administrative capacity to implement an air quality modeling program; helped the Mexican government carry out other technical studies; and assisted in the modernization of industrial plants and the purchase and installation of air pollution control equipment.

In 1992, Canada and Mexico embarked on a series of cooperative efforts to assist in environmental capacity building. Under this initiative, the Canadians provided Mexico with equipment and training for monitoring air quality, technical advice on managing industrial and other wastes, advice on controlling other forms of pollution, and assistance in implementing environmental impact studies.

WORLD BANK

Over the mid- to late 1990s, Mexico relied on World Bank funding for a wide variety of government spending programs, including those aimed at increasing environmental capacity and promoting good governance. Mexico accounts for the second largest share of the World Bank's disbursed and outstanding portfolio, totaling $11.1 billion—9.4 percent of the World Bank's total portfolio. The World Bank's loans to Mexico from July 1997 to June 2000 totaled about $3.9 billion for 13 projects. In addition, the CEC is in the process of tapping into Global Environment Facility funds, which are managed jointly by the World Bank and the United Nations.

The World Bank's assistance strategy for Mexico was updated in June 1999, when the bank's executive board provided for loans of $5.2 billion up to 2001 to be used for improving social conditions for Mexico's poor; for reinforcing macroeconomic stability; and for strengthening public governance reforms, including loans to decentralize Mexico's public administration. The World Bank's environmental strategy aims to strengthen the environmental ministry's institutional capacity and to support the decentralization of environmental services and infrastructure development, transferring these responsibilities to Mexico's states and municipalities. Bank loans also are used to expand Mexico's air quality program in Mexico City; to continue support for phasing out ozone-depleting substances under the Montreal Protocol; and to deepen the dialogue between government and private industry, leading to a consensus on approaches to decreasing industrial pollution and strengthening environmental management systems. Mexico also uses World Bank loans to support irrigated agriculture and groundwater stabilization, to assist local forestry communities that are attempting in implementing sustainable resource management, and to expand partnerships with the Global Environment Facility.

Recent or ongoing activities supported by the World Bank and designed for environmental capacity building span the range of the bank's lending instruments. For example, a recent Decentralization Adjustment Loan includes an innovative component for federal transfers of funds allocated specifically to environmental capacity building at the state level in Mexico. This program, which began in 1999, represents a significant step toward effective decentralization of environmental management, because it gives state governments direct control over the funds. Another, more traditional approach to capacity building is included in the World Bank-supported Northern Border Environment Program, in which the *Secretaría de Medio Ambiente y Recursos Naturales* (Semarnat, including its deconcentrated *delegaciones*) is managing the funds allocated for state and municipal environmental capacity building.

Building on lessons learned, the World Bank is assisting Mexico in exploring the use of economic instruments for environmentally sustainable development policies. Bank activities include an analysis of linkages between key sector policies and the environment. The World Bank, in conjunction with Mexican institutions, is identifying a range of policy interventions that would integrate environmental protection and sustainable development objectives.

The discussion of North American economic integration and other, more global influences shows that these outside influences have heightened Mexico's interest in certain environmental management concepts. Therefore, the analysis that follows will focus on a series of management tools that any given government uses in the development of national environmental policy. The Mexican government's ability or inability to use these management tools will be described in some detail.

Note

[1] United Nations, Global Environment Facility, "Project Performance Report 2000," GEF Council Publication no. GEF/C-17/8, April 10, 2001; available at www.un.org (August 4, 2001).

CHAPTER SIX

ADOPTING ENVIRONMENTAL MANAGEMENT TOOLS

EACH TIME THE MEXICAN GOVERNMENT INITIATES A CRISIS RESPONSE to resource depletion or environmental degradation, significant obstacles have to be surmounted. The government's ability to overcome these obstacles is directly related to its managerial capacity as well as to the level of national financial challenges that the government must face. Mexico has made many changes in its environmental programs over the past five years, but questions remain as to how many management tools and techniques the government has been able to adopt effectively to deal with challenges. In each of the three serious environmental challenges Mexico has experienced since the 1980s, the government's initial responses reflected the following:

- lack of information on the rate of environmental or natural resource deterioration, because monitoring systems were not in place;
- lack of information on the economic effects of environmental or natural resource deterioration,
- the need to establish a methodology and an implementation plan to mitigate the damage;
- lack of technical training and experience in dealing with the problem;
- insufficient financial resources to deal with the problem;
- lack of regional and municipal commitment to carry out federal mandates; and

- an initial failure to inform the public and to include civil society in the decisionmaking involved in mitigating the crisis.

This chapter explores the extent to which Mexico has been able to effectively adopt management tools that will be useful not only in dealing with environmental crises but also in reaching the government's stated goals for sustainable development.

FUNDING

Mexico's environmental budget expands and contracts with economic cycles, and the government has been modernizing its budgeting process by attempting to link budget outlays more closely to performance measures. The federal environmental program faced serious limitations in carrying out its mandate from 1986 through 1989, the period when the Mexican economy was recovering from the 1982 financial crisis. The federal government reduced public-sector expenditures and weakened several federal ministries that controlled social programs. The World Bank reported that, between 1986 and 1989, Mexico's environmental operating budget declined 69 percent in real terms, and salaries for higher-level permanent staff fell 50 percent.[1]

The financial crisis of the 1980s contributed to the severity of Mexico's environmental problems, in large measure because both government programs and infrastructure investments lagged during this period. As part of its fiscal reforms since that crisis, Mexico has made a concerted effort to reduce fiscal deficits—from 15 percent of the gross domestic product (GDP) in 1987 to 1.2 percent in 1998—and this has lessened inflationary pressures. However, the reduction in fiscal deficits also drastically reduced the amount of money available for social programs, including environmental protection.

From 1986 through 1989, the environmental subsecretariat of the *Secretaría de Desarrollo Urbano y Ecología* (Sedue) lost about 25 percent of its permanent staff, 20 percent of its telephones, and 35 percent of its functioning vehicles. The economic crisis in the 1980s also affected investment in irrigation infrastructure, which is now neglected and substandard, and contributed to Mexico's water shortage and energy use. In many cases, the lack of funding halted or slowed down the implementation of environmental regulations or programs that had been planned when Mexico promulgated a broad range of technical standards in 1988.

For example, in the late 1980s and early 1990s, Sedue established a nationwide network of 402 stations that monitor water quality. The office had also intended to implement a monitoring plan that called for collecting samples from these stations each month and for analyzing 20 basic parameters of water quality, including dissolved oxygen, acidity, suspended particulates, sulfates, and fecal coliform counts. But by 1992, Sedue was still unable to implement the monitoring program because of insufficient material, equipment, and trained personnel.[2]

Environmental funding began to recover in 1990, when the operational budget was 30 percent higher in real terms than it had been in 1989. That same year, as Mexico began seeking free-trade negotiations with the United States and as an intense U.S. debate began on Mexico's environmental performance, the Salinas administration began pouring financial resources into the environmental budget and forcing state-owned industries to make capital investments in pollution control equipment, technology, and modernization of emissions management techniques.

By 1991, the government estimated that total public and private environmental investment was about $1.8 billion—or almost 0.7 percent of GDP—and the Salinas administration vowed that private-sector environmental investment and expenditures would increase 15 percent annually for the foreseeable future.[3] Because Mexico lacked the financial resources to pay this environmental cost, loans from the World Bank and other institutions supplied a portion of the financing not only for modernization of state-owned industries but also for the budget of the Ministry of Social Development (*Secretaría de Desarrollo Social,* Sedesol). (See table 6.1.) Of the $78.169 million spent in 1992, $24.371 million came from World Bank loans and $4.795 million from other loans[4]

In the wake of the December 1994 peso devaluation, however, the budgets of federal programs were again reduced substantially, and

Table 6.1
Sedesol Budgets by Funding Source, 1988–1992
(in millions of U.S. dollars)

Budget Year	Federal Funds	World Bank Funds	Other Loans	Total Budget
1988	$4.269	—	—	$4.269
1989	$6.580	—	—	$6.580
1990	$11.768	—	—	$11.768
1991	$10.615	$18.093	$9.776	$38.484
1992	$49.003	$24.371	$4.795	$78.169

Sources: Secretaría de Desarrollo Social (Sedesol), *Informe de Labores, 1986–1987* (Mexico City, 1988); Sedesol, *Informe de Labores, 1988-1989* (Mexico City, 1990); Sedesol, Instituto Nacional de Ecología, *México: Informe de la Situación General en Materia de Equilibrio Ecológico y Protección al Ambiente, 1993–1994* (Mexico City, April 1994).

they remained at modest levels through the end of the decade,[5] as the data in table 6.2 indicate. The table shows the value of the budget for the environmental ministry (*Secretaría de Medio Ambiente y Recursos Naturales,* Semarnat) in 1995 pesos. In current pesos, unadjusted for inflation, Semarnat's budget was also a modest part of the overall programmable budget, as table 6.3 shows. The data in tables 6.2 and 6.3 are not directly comparable because the accounting methods used to identify the budget figures vary.

In 2001, Mexico's environmental budget did not shrink, but most environmental officials believe that it is insufficient to address some of the nation's most pressing natural resource problems. In a June 2001 interview with the Mexican press, Secretary of the Environment Victor Lichtinger said that the federal budget assigned to environmental protection was so low it could be interpreted as not assigning appropriate importance to the protection of natural resources.[6] The Fox administration proposed a series of fiscal reforms that would increase tax revenues by more than 2 percent of GDP, and some of the increased revenue would likely flow into environmental programs.

Table 6.2
Semarnat Budgets, 1995–2000
(in millions of 1995 pesos)

Year	Secretariat	Profepa & Ecology & Fisheries Institutes	National Water Commission	Total
1995	4.2	1.0	3.5	8.7
1996	5.0	1.2	4.4	10.6
1997	6.0	1.5	5.0	12.5
1998	5.8	1.6	5.3	12.7
1999	5.7	1.6	5.1	12.4
2000	5.6	1.8	4.8	12.2

Source: Adapted by author from data available in Ministry of the Environment, Natural Resources and Fisheries (Semarnat), *Mexico: Policies to Promote Sustainable Development* (Mexico City, April 2000).

Note: Numbers are rounded; they cannot be compared directly to Sedesol budget detailed in table 6.1 because of changes in institutions and accounting methods.

However, the Mexican Congress rejected many of President Fox's proposals. In addition, over the first two years of President Fox's administration, the economy did not grow as anticipated, prompting reductions to the federal budget. As a result, the 2001 budget for Semarnat dropped slightly from the amount allocated in 2000. In September 2002, President Fox announced that federal revenues continued to be lower than expected, and he proposed that Mexico adopt an austere budget for 2003 that would cut public-sector spending, and therefore reduce the public-sector deficit from 0.65 to 0.5 percent.[7]

In spite of continuing funding shortfalls at the time, in November 2000, environmental ministry officials said that they were moving forward to adopt parts of the U.S. budgeting process by linking medium- and long-term planning to potential funding sources, but this is hard to do in Mexico, which uses only a one-year budgeting process. Mexico's periodic financial crises that affect public-sector

Table 6.3
Semarnat Share of Mexico's Federal Budget, 1995–2000
(in millions of current pesos)

Year	Federal Budget	Semarnat/-Programmable Budget	Percent of Semarnap Budget	Federal Budget	Percent of Programmable Budget
1995	453,930	290,423	4,221	0.93%	1.45%
1996	609,329	403,449	6,725	1.10%	1.67%
1997	776,306	528,123	10,198	1.31%	1.93%
1998	858,380	600,583	12,525	1.46%	2.09%
1999	1,015,610	711,228	13,315	1.31%	1.87%
2000	1,187,819	816,734	14,520	1.22%	1.78%

Source: Compiled by author from information contained in North American Commission for Environmental Cooperation, "Priorities for Reinforcing Management Capacities in Mexico," Montreal, June 2001; and author's telephone interviews with Semarnat officials, November 5, 2002.
Note: Numbers are rounded.

spending also hamper the ministry's budgeting. Like its U.S. counterparts, Semarnat's planning staff is developing a linked system of planning, budgeting, programming, assessment, and evaluation, under which budgeting is tied to performance measures.

HUMAN CAPITAL

Efficient management systems depend in part on the training, experience, and level of employee competence. Implementation of Mexico's ambitious environmental program often has been slowed since the 1980s, because federal environmental agencies under various presidential administrations have struggled with small staffs and high turnover rates. Because of low pay scales, the federal government tends to hire people with little experience and then train them. Once trained, these employees promptly leave for higher-paying jobs in the private sector. This turnover greatly inhibits any given environmental program's capacity to carry out its mandates.

One example is in air quality. In 1992, the environmental ministry, Sedue, was responsible for inspecting about 15,000 firms in the Mexico City Metropolitan Area. To carry out this mission, Sedue had only 9 trained inspectors (3 for wastewater, 4 for atmospheric emissions, and 2 for noise). Throughout the rest of the country, Sedue had 66 inspectors to cover about 40,000 firms.[8]

By 2000, given Mexico's fiscal policy of limiting public-sector expenditures, environmental officials were still complaining about significant staff shortages across all programs. One of the most seriously affected agencies was Mexico's Office of the Federal Attorney General for Environmental Protection (Profepa). In 2001, Profepa inspectors earned the equivalent of $270 to $850 per month, depending on experience, and the office's 25 lawyers handled several hundred legal challenges each year.[9] Profepa's inspection branch has only 400 inspectors to monitor natural resources—from beaches to forests. Yet deforestation, water quality and quantity, erosion, and loss of biodiversity are Mexico's most serious concerns.

Since 1980, various United Nations agencies, as well as the U.S., Canadian, and Japanese governments, have sponsored seminars to train environmental personnel in air quality management, environmental compliance and enforcement, management of protected areas and endangered species, and other areas designated as priorities in Mexico's environmental management program. The number of training seminars and courses increased again with the implementation of the 1992 U.S.-Mexican border plan and gained even more intensity after the signing of the North American Free Trade Agreement (NAFTA) and the establishment of the North American Commission for Environmental Cooperation (CEC).

By the end of the Zedillo administration, a number of environmental ministry officials had shifted their focus from training midlevel professional staff in natural resource program management to searching for more advanced economic training in the use of economic instruments for environmental initiatives, methods of incorporating environmental indicators into GDP, and methodologies for implementing risk assessments and developing risk reduction strategies.

ENVIRONMENTAL REGULATIONS

Before 1992, Mexico had no federal governmental unit dedicated specifically to enforcement of environmental regulations. The establishment of the Office of the Federal Attorney General for Environmental Protection was a turning point in the country's environmental management, but the move has not ended long-standing problems of weak enforcement of environmental policies. The limitations to Profepa's effectiveness include regulatory jurisdiction that overlaps with that of other federal agencies, a continuing lack of data on industrial emissions, insufficient budget and personnel, and a lack of both political will and management capacity at state and local levels.

Much of Mexico's enforcement regime is the result of international pressures. Some Profepa officials believe that the creation of their office in 1992 was almost an outgrowth of both Mexico's participation in the 1992 Rio Conference on Environment and Development and the political battles the government waged on its environmental record during negotiations for a free-trade agreement with the United States and Canada. Thus, many officials believed that part of the continuing strong resistance to compliance with environmental laws relating to industries or land use laws in the agricultural sector stems from the fact that an enforcement regime came before the Mexican public had effectively demanded one.

EARLY YEARS

Mexico began an enforcement campaign several years before Profepa was established, partly in response to complaints about the environmental deterioration in Mexico's northern border region, where Mexican subsidiaries of U.S. companies were straining the urban infrastructure. However, complaints also surfaced from Mexico City residents and a group of intellectual and artists who called themselves the Group of 100.

In the late 1980s, U.S. demands rose substantially for better Mexican management of industries in its northern border region, many of which were U.S.-owned. As demands for action rose, the Mexican government had few technical regulations governing industry's activities or setting limits to industrial emissions. Nevertheless, Sedue officials conducted some well-publicized inspections and industrial plant shutdowns, often without warning and with very little due process preceding the shutdown. Every few months, the shutdowns were accompanied by a public tabulation of the number of inspections and shutdowns, and this running tabulation received substantial attention in Mexico City's newspapers. But efforts to force corporations to alter their environmental behavior increased substantially just at the time NAFTA negotiations began.

From the time President Salinas de Gortari took office in December 1988 up to September 1992, the federal government took several steps:

- It suspended the operating licenses of 1,926 facilities and closed them down for noncompliance with environmental regulations.
- It permanently closed down more than 100 facilities in the Mexico City area at a cost of $500 million in government revenues.
- It increased the number of environmental inspectors from fewer than 100 to 300.
- It forced 2,112 industries to install pollution control equipment.
- It inspected more than 7,668 industrial sites.[10]

Profepa began operations in 1992 with a media splash during the NAFTA debate. Inspectors started by conducting 4,380 complete inspections of industrial facilities and 375 "brief visits." These inspections aimed to identify irregularities, order corrective actions, and impose fines when appropriate. The actions appeared to have more publicity value than substance, however, because Mexico had few technical environmental regulations to enforce and few trained inspectors.[11]

Table 6.4
Profepa Inspections, 1992–1997

Year	Complete Visits	Brief Inspections
1992	4,380	375
1993	8,699	7,054
1994	9,514	3,388
1995	12,881	No data
1996	13,324	No data
1997	11,761	No data

Sources:Secretaria de Medio Ambiente, Recursos Naturales y Pesca (Semarnap), Procuraduría Federal de Protección al Ambiente (Profepa), *Informe Trianual, 1995–1997,* 2nd ed. (Mexico City, 1998); Semarnap, *La Gestión Ambiental en México* (Mexico City, October 2000); and Semarnap, Profepa, *La Auditoría Ambiental en México* (Mexico City, 2000).

After 1992, the number of serious infractions decreased significantly, leading Profepa officials to speculate that industries were taking compliance seriously. But actual evidence is sketchy, because Profepa inspectors were not well trained; environmental regulation was limited; and Mexico's newspapers contained numerous accounts of inspectors who had been threatened, assaulted, or prohibited access to industry facilities. Additionally, the federal government is not responsible for enforcing all categories of environmental law, and Profepa primarily monitors government-owned industries.

After 1994, just as NAFTA was implemented, the brief visits tapered off and the federal government published few statistics on its enforcement actions. (See table 6.4.) Instead, the government concentrated on more thorough and professional inspections that drew less attention. In all, 69,076 inspections of industry were made from August 1992 through December 1997. From these inspections, Profepa found 2,340 serious infractions of environmental laws and 51,921 minor infractions; no violations were detected in the course of 14,815 inspections.[12]

Table 6.5
Profepa Inspections, All Categories, 1997–2000

Year	Total Inspections
1997	12,240
1998	9,590
1999	8,671
2000	7,600

Source: Adapted from Semarnap, *Mexico: Policies to Promote Sustainable Development.*

The well-publicized inspections at first appeared to be more for the sake of international publicity than for actual enforcement, because Mexico did not establish many of its fixed-source emission limits until 1993 or 1994. In fact, Profepa officials conceded that their industrial inspections in the early 1990s had focused only on administrative procedures and not on technical verification of emissions, leaks, or other technical issues, because the organization lacked the laboratory capacity to analyze environmental samples.

Many of the plant shutdowns were partial and lasted for only a few hours or a few days; penalties for environmental infractions were not substantial. The number of plant closures decreased over time, but the number of fines and penalties that were assessed increased. For the three-year period between 1995 and 1997, Profepa closed 568 facilities completely and 206 partially. However, inspections of another 28,647 facilities resulted in fines or penalties, and no penalties were assessed after visits to 9,319 facilities. Nevertheless, the inspections had the effect of capturing the attention of Mexican industries, and the visits solidified the federal government's perceived right to control environmental impacts caused by industrial activities.

Inspections continued to increase for several years, until NAFTA was implemented, although the publicity began to decrease. (See table 6.5.) In 1993–1994, Profepa conducted 20,554 industrial inspections to monitor fixed sources of pollution,[13] and inspectors made another 2,614 visits to natural protected areas to enforce environmental regulations.

The federal government consolidated and streamlined its enforcement functions in 1995, and the environmental ministry's enforcement arm began to more closely resemble programs in other industrialized countries. Profepa was given new responsibilities for enforcing all regulations governing the use of natural resources. Before that change, these responsibilities had been dispersed among several government ministries, including the agricultural secretariat.

The large number of industry inspections from 1992 through 1997 can be attributed to an initial phase during which the federal government asserted its newfound authority to inspect industries and demand compliance with environmental laws. Much of this enforcement effort, however, was directed at state-owned industries and at multinational firms in Mexico's northern region that shares a border with the United States. By 1996, the number of inspections that found serious violations of environmental law had dropped—from about 20 percent in 1992 to just 1.78 percent—and continued to remain low, totaling only 1.5 percent of visits in 2000.

In 1997, the *Secretaría de Medio Ambiente, Recursos Naturales y Pesca* (Semarnap) began to simplify and streamline its permitting process for certain industries by combining multiple permits into a single environmental license. The goal was to substitute other operating licenses for this single license. To obtain the license, a business was required to comply with all regulations relating to environmental impact, risk assessments, emissions, and hazardous waste. The one-stop licensing has not been well utilized: only 1 environmental license was issued in 1997, 52 were issued in 1998, and 73 in 1999. Semarnap also continued to issue other types of operating licenses to industries. These licenses peaked at more than 2,000 in 1994 but dwindled to just 102 by 1999.[14]

The federal government changed gears again in 1998, with a decision to decrease the number of industry inspections and to concentrate, instead, on an enforcement strategy under which fewer, but more thorough, inspections of facilities would be conducted. Profepa began to do so, using an indexing system designed to ensure that specific industries complied with the technical regulations appropriate to that industry.

Current Enforcement Strategy

Mexico's current environmental enforcement strategy is based on four programs: industrial inspections, environmental audits, inspection and surveillance of the use of natural resources, and citizen denouncement of environmental crimes.[15] Profepa's future priorities are to augment the number of inspectors it has and to obtain legal changes that will give the agency full powers to conduct criminal prosecutions. At present, local authorities are responsible for criminal prosecution of environmental crimes, and the ability to carry out that function varies significantly. To accomplish these tasks, Profepa officials said they need more funding. Miguel Angel Cancino, Profepa's legal director, pointed out that, in real pesos, Profepa's budget is no higher than it was in 1995.[16]

CEC's Influence on Mexican Enforcement

The CEC attempts to enhance enforcement of environmental regulations in all three NAFTA countries not only through its process of investigating citizens' complaints about a government's failure to enforce its own environmental laws but also through projects aimed at improving industry compliance, determining the level of industry's environmental performance, and training government inspectors. About one-third of the CEC money spent on enforcement projects is allotted to training seminars and projects, particularly in the areas of wildlife and forestry practices.

Continuing Enforcement Challenges

Profepa officials said that they are determined to strengthen their authority to conduct criminal prosecutions of environmental crimes, and they have the support of some Mexican environmentalists in this effort. Criminal prosecution currently falls under the purview of the Office of the Federal Attorney General for Environmental Protection, but such cases are hard to prove. The federal prosecutor's office has failed to win convictions in several cases of animal trafficking, for example, because the law requires proof that the animals in question are for commercial use. Other environmental criminals, such as clandestine loggers who work under the protection of armed guards, can be apprehended only when Profepa has access to armed police.

In the United States, lawsuits brought by private citizens regularly force government officials to punish environmental violators even when it might be more politically expedient to overlook their activities; both Profepa officials and environmental attorneys in Mexico would like to develop that culture in Mexico. Many environmentalists, believing that the courts are the weakest link in Mexico's enforcement system, say that judges often do no know environmental law or the way to apply it in specific cases. At least one environmental group in Mexico City offers legal seminars on environmental law for the government's judicial branch. Until criminal prosecution procedures can be standardized in Mexico, however, some environmentalists say that much of Mexico's enforcement will continue to be politically driven.[17]

Profepa officials complained that their office has jurisdictional disputes with the semiautonomous National Water Commission, which limit Profepa's authority to enforce water pollution laws. For example, Profepa's mandate does not extend to the discharge of hazardous waste into federal waters; Profepa permit inspectors cannot monitor this or water-recycling programs.

The ambiguous relationship between federal and local enforcement also complicates Profepa's job. Much enforcement, from garbage to land use planning, falls under local jurisdiction. But Profepa's legal director has said that only Mexico City and 12 of the country's 31 states have rewritten their environmental laws to bring them into compliance with the 1996 strengthening of the federal law.[18]

Profepa officials said they would like more decentralization of enforcement programs but are concerned about the lack of political will at the local level to develop or enforce environmental regulations. According to Profepa, some state governments are actually hostile to enforcement, as reflected in the fact that at least three Profepa inspectors have been killed on the job.

The Public's Role in Enforcement

Article 199 of Mexico's 1988 omnibus environmental act contained a provision encouraging public participation in activities designed to protect the environment, but until the creation of Profepa, the public had few mechanisms for interacting with government officials on these issues. In 1992, Profepa established a complaint unit, whose goal was to reinforce environmental compliance by creating a culture of environmentalism. In early 2001, Secretary of the Environment Victor Lichtinger reinforced this mechanism by establishing an office within Semarnat to deal specifically with the provision of public information.

The number of complaints filed with Profepa has steadily increased over time. In 1992, the first year of the complaint program, 1,321 complaints were filed. From 1992 through 1994, Profepa received 12,162 complaints; and from 1995 through 1997, the office received 17,200. Of the complaints filed from 1995 through 1997, 30.45 percent were about air pollution, 23.45 percent about forestry issues, 21.75 percent about wildlife management, and 14.53 percent about land use practices; another 8.59 percent were about the quality or availability of water.[19]

Of the complaints filed from 1992 through 1997, in Profepa's judgment, 53 percent were successfully resolved after Profepa's investigation, and 16 percent were deemed improper complaints or complaints about issues outside Profepa's jurisdiction. Profepa found no violation of environmental law in 16 percent of these cases and made recommendations for resolving the complaint in 2 percent of the cases.[20]

Clean Industry Audits

By l994, Mexico had developed a new enforcement instrument—environmental audits—that could lead to granting a Clean Industries certificate, which essentially guaranteed that the government would leave a firm alone for at least one year. The audit program, the essential element in Mexico's Clean Industries Program, runs on a parallel track to other verification and inspection programs. The Clean Industries Program actually is an outgrowth of a 1993 auditing program that was less rigorous. Although Clean Industries certification extends only to Mexico's largest facilities, which are located primarily in central and northern Mexico, Profepa officials have said that they plan to extend the program to smaller industries.

Sedesol's 1994 annual report indicated that the voluntary audit program was established in part because the Mexican government had been impressed with similar programs operating in other countries.[21] The aim of this program is pollution prevention—to analyze a facility's procedures and practices to determine whether any corrective or preventive practices can be incorporated into industrial processes. Emissions into air, water, and groundwater are analyzed as part of this process. Once a facility is certified under the program, it is allowed to self-report its emissions and performance data. In return, Profepa agrees not to make random inspections of the facility for the term of the one-year certification.

Mr. Lichtinger believes that, over the past five years, this approach has generated a dramatic change in attitude among large companies, because many large firms and multinational firms are now using the audits to comply with environmental regulations. Profepa is now expanding the audit procedure, incorporating issues relating to the health of local communities. In a 1997 survey of 236 Mexican industrial firms, 60 percent of officials surveyed said their primary motivation for good environmental performance was to implement environmental regulations. Internal company policies relating to the environment also accounted for more than 50 percent of the motivation to improve environmental performance, and local community opinion accounted for 25 percent.[22]

To gain a Clean Industries certificate, a facility must undergo a complete environmental assessment of its operations. As part of the audit, facility managers must agree to and implement an action plan to correct any deficiencies that inhibit the ability to comply with federal environmental standards, and sometimes the facilities must meet higher international standards. These corrective actions, which typically must be taken within one to four years, can include repairs, installation of antipollution equipment, changes in operating procedures, or other measures. Profepa officials say that facilities with Clean Industries certification generally have to make some capital investment in new pollution equipment, but most often they realize a substantial cost reduction in energy, materials used, and insurance, as well as reductions in on-the-job accidents once their facilities are operating according to specified action plans.

After a facility has complied with its action plan, it is issued a Clean Industries certificate, which is valid for one year and can be renewed. From 1992 through 1997, 896 environmental audits were conducted in both state-owned and private facilities, including *Petróleos Mexicanos* (Pemex) facilities as well as those belonging to General Motors, Nissan, Ford, Cervecería Cuauhtemoc, Cervecería Modelo, Grupo Acerero del Norte, Ciba Geigy, and Nestle. Apparently, no Clean Industries certificates were awarded until 1997.[23] In 1997, 115 certificates were awarded, and another 122 were awarded in 1998. From 1997 through 1999, a total of 421 industries received the Clean Industries certificate, and 16 were in the process of being certified.[24] As of July 2000, 527 companies had received certification.

Profepa conceded that only large industries are the ones to agree to the environmental audits, and many of these are state-owned industries over which Profepa has more political leverage. Before the initiation of the Clean Industry Program, a number of less rigorous audits began in 1992 in the Coatzacoalcos-Minatitlan industrial corridor. The 66 audits conducted in 1993 covered the cement, mining, chemical, pharmaceutical, and paper industries and included facilities belonging to Pemex, the national railroad, and Cemex (a leading cement and ready-mix concrete producer), among others.

As of June 2000, Profepa had completed 1,393 environmental audits, but only about 300 domestic and international facilities had gone through the extra environmental measures recommended beyond what was required for certification.[25] Although these represented only about 10 percent of Mexican industry, they also accounted for the largest production facilities in Mexico. By Semarnap's calculations, these facilities produced about 60 percent of Mexico's industrial GDP. Data gathered by the commerce and trade ministry (*Secretaría de Comercio y Fomento Industrial,* Secofi) indicate that, within Mexico's private sector, at least half of the value added in manufacturing occurs among a handful of large domestic and multinational firms. But the other half of Mexico's manufacturing is generated by a series of micro-, small-, and medium-sized enterprises, which have never been well regulated in Mexico. In addition, federal regulations often do not extend to micro-industries.

Economic Reforms and Their Effect on Compliance

The measure that has helped Mexico improve management of some of its most polluting sectors in the 1990s was a massive campaign to privatize those industries when permitted under the Mexican Constitution. In 1988, the Mexican government operated 618 state-owned facilities, but with the privatization that occurred with the opening up of Mexico's economy, by 1994 that number had dwindled to 257.[26]

The reduced number of facilities also made it easier for Semarnap, with its scarce resources, to inspect and audit these sites. In addition, in 1993–1994, Semarnap initiated a regulatory crackdown on Pemex, in tandem with a reorganization of the giant state-owned firm, forcing it to begin a capital investment program in more energy-efficient equipment and environmental control equipment.[27] At about the same time, the Mexican government also began to push its electricity-generating sector to switch to cleaner burning natural gas, but Pemex's limited ability to produce and transport gas to needed urban areas has hampered this effort.

ECONOMIC INSTRUMENTS

By its own assessment, Mexico is not taking advantage of many economic instruments to reach its environmental management goals. Even though the government has officially adopted the "polluter-pays principle" as part of its obligations under the Organization for Economic Cooperation and Development (OECD), in practice, the polluter does not bear the environmental costs of doing business. In 1994, Semarnap identified six types of economic instruments and conceded that it had mastered only one partially. (These are listed in table 6.6.)

Mexico strengthened its omnibus environmental law in 1996 and adopted some economic measures to achieve the government's environmental and resource management objectives. These measures are

Table 6.6
Mexico's Assessment of Its Use of Economic Instruments, 1994

Instrument	Use
Emission charges	Very limited wastewater charges
Product charges	Tax on used automobile sales
Industrial or commercial permits	None
Deposit refunds	Not used for environmental purposes
Tradable permits	None
Performance bonds for environmental damage	Limited to nuclear damage

Sources: Compiled from data available in Semarnap, *La Gestión Ambiental en México;* Marcelo M. Giugale, Olivier Lafourcade, and Vinh H. Nguyen, eds., *Mexico: A Comprehensive Development Agenda for the New Era* (Washington, D.C.: International Bank for Reconstruction and Development, World Bank, April 2001); and author's interviews with Semarnap staff, Mexico City, November 2000.

limited and not well utilized, however. For example, although a gasoline surcharge was instituted for the Mexico City area, the government stopped collecting the fees in 1998. Of the few measures adopted, state-owned industries appear to be the most affected. For example, since 1996, Pemex has been required to post bonds for potential environmental damage of up to 30 percent of contract value.[28]

Mexico has made progress in promoting the functioning of water markets in the 1990s. But water supply is heavily subsidized in Mexico, and these subsidies must be eliminated. Likewise, state and municipal governments have little direct revenue from taxes and almost no ability to assess user fees. Local and regional governments have almost no incentive for collecting taxes or for recovering costs expended for environmental services. Many local water utility companies were created in the late 1980s and early 1990s, but these entities do not pay water extraction fees or pollution taxes, and most are unable to comply with Mexican or international environmental standards.

Pollution charges have been in place in Mexico since 1991, but they have proved difficult to enforce.[29] Mexico's water law allows the National Water Commission to apply the polluter-pays principle on water discharge from municipalities and industrial plants that exceed certain standards for organic matter and suspended solids. Lack of enforcement has substantially reduced the revenue raised by these charges, however. In 1997, World Bank researchers determined that the program was failing because of poor monitoring and opposition from polluters.[30] In 2001, the Fox administration recommended that the Mexican Congress implement a fiscal reform package that would give the federal government more flexibility in using economic instruments to direct consumer and industrial behavior toward the nation's sustainable development goals, but the Congress failed to approve most of President Fox's proposals.

ENVIRONMENTAL ASSESSMENTS

Environmental assessments are one of the most important policy tools for systematically determining how an activity or set of activities will affect the environment, thus integrating development and environmental policies. The assessments can be used at the local, national, or global level—wherever economic, environmental, and social development goals need to be reconciled. The use of environmental assessments as a planning tool is relatively recent in Mexico, and the country's environmentalists are calling for additional changes that would extend the types of development projects that would require such assessments.

Sustainability Assessments

Sustainability assessment is a term used to describe the process of assessing the potential environmental impacts of economic growth that is spurred by increased trade and foreign investment. On the global level, in 1999, the European Union developed a "Sustainability Impact Assessment" methodology to analyze the development impacts of

World Trade Organization measures that were expected to emanate from a new round of trade talks.

A number of international environmental organizations have called for a sustainability assessment of the Free Trade Area of the Americas plan while the agreement is being negotiated in order to identify both positive and negative social and ecological impacts of increased trade and investment.[31] Environmentalists want the sustainability process to culminate in a series of detailed recommendations both on the specific environmental language to be incorporated into the trade agreement and on the specific environmental cooperation process that should be developed to support a sustainable trade regime for the hemisphere. However, the ability of nations throughout the hemisphere to collect and analyze the data needed to assess likely environmental deterioration resulting from trade-related economic growth is likely to vary substantially. Many of these countries have little experience in using environmental impact assessments on individual development projects.

Environmental Impact Assessments

Environmental impact assessments are evaluations of the ecological effects of proposed public or private activities. In Mexico, these assessments are used to determine if the environmental impacts of proposed projects fall within limits set by the government's environmental regulations. Projects can be modified or rejected if the environmental impacts are deemed to be inappropriately damaging.

The Mexican government published its first regulation on environmental impact assessments and risk assessments shortly after the general ecology law went into effect in 1988. Initially, only the impacts of the largest public and private projects were assessed, and the World Bank declared that the quality of these assessments was often inadequate.

Mexico began using environmental impact assessments in the late 1980s. (See table 6.7.) From 1988 through 1990, the government evaluated 600 forest projects and 934 other projects; in 1990, it evaluated 511 projects.[32] However, assessments of industrial projects were limited. From 1988 through 1990, federal authorities undertook

Table 6.7
Mexico's Use of Environmental Impact Assessments, 1989–1992

Year	Number of Impact Assessments	Number of Risk Assessments
1989	71	86
1990	338	102
1991	269	89
1992	375	44

Sources: Secretaría de Desarrollo Social,, "Protección del Medio Ambiente, Acciones," Mexico City, June 5, 1993; and Ministry of Urban Development and Ecology (Sedue), "Aspects of Mexico's Environmental Policy and the Environmental Situation in Mexico," Mexico City, April 1991.

industrial assessments on only 19 chemical plants, 3 iron and steel plants and foundries, 1 petrochemical plant, 1 tannery, 2 oil pipelines, and 8 electric power plants.

Between the 1991–1992 fiscal year and the following biennium, the number of projects undergoing environmental impact assessments rose by 66.9 percent.[33] The number continued to rise, but government evaluations were slow and clumsy, leading to tensions with state-owned industries. In the 1993–1994 fiscal year, 1,507 impact assessments submitted to the government were rejected, representing a rejection rate of 66.5 percent.[34]

Despite the complaints, in 1996, as part of a general strengthening of environmental law, Mexico expanded the types of activities for which an environmental impact assessment is required. In addition, environmental impact assessments are now used in conjunction with regional land use plans to evaluate the environmental effects of projects and the adequacy of mitigation measures.

In conducting environmental impact assessments, Mexican law requires Semarnap to take into account entire ecosystems, not only those resources that are exploited or affected. Depending on the impact that an undertaking may have on the ecosystem or on public health and depending on the likelihood that the proposed project will violate environmental law, the government can require three types of environmental assessments: (1) a preventive report, (2) an environmental impact statement, or (3) a risk study in cases where hazardous undertakings are proposed. The government uses the results of these assessments as an enforcement tool. After reviewing an environmental impact statement, Semarnat can authorize the work without conditions, establish additional preventive and mitigation measures for the project, modify the project' or deny the requested authorization.

Environmental Risk Assessments

In Mexico, environmental risk assessments are undertaken for certain high-risk activities that may pose a danger either to ecosystems or to public health. In general, these activities include the management or production of flammable materials and the use of explosives, toxic chemicals, radioactive materials, and other corrosive or biologically harmful materials. The federal government published initial lists of such activities in 1990 and again in 1992; in 1994, it published regulations governing how risk assessments should be conducted.

From 1989 through 1992, 321 risk assessments were submitted to Sedesol. The use of risk assessments continued to rise in the wake of a 1992 gas explosion in Guadalajara, an event that spurred the government to require some 315 risk assessments in the 1993–1994 fiscal year; 268 of those submitted were approved.

DECENTRALIZATION OF ENVIRONMENTAL MANAGEMENT

The inability of many Latin American and Caribbean governments to decentralize budgetary and policy implementation authority, transferring it to state and local governments, sets substantial limits on these governments' ability to carry out national policy and to address local environmental issues. Federal agencies in these countries are too centralized and too remote to adequately address local environmental issues; and state and local governments—like federal governments—must build environmental capacity before they can carry out federal mandates.

For several decades, the Mexican government has had a stated goal of decentralizing many kinds of decisionmaking to state governments, and each presidential administration since the 1970s has made some attempt to decentralize some of its authority. Most of Mexico's national development plans over the past 30 years have set decentralization as a goal. Under the de la Madrid administration, some *municipios* were granted fixed sources of revenue. Under the Salinas administration, pilot projects were designed to help certain local governments collect user revenue for municipal services like garbage collection. The Zedillo administration undertook a pilot decentralization project for the state of Guanajuato.[35]

In the 1990s, Mexico set in motion the decentralization of legal authority to state and local governments so that these entities could operate their own environmental management programs. By 1992, 29 of the 31 Mexican states—all except Tlaxcala and Campeche—had some environmental legislation.[36] As of 1994, Semarnap recognized 8 state governments out of 31 that had developed adequate state laws for land use planning and natural resource management.[37]

Mexico's environmental officials envision three parts to environmental decentralization to state and local governments: legal reforms, fiscal reforms, and regional capacity building to implement environmental management programs. The legal reforms for decentralization are mostly in place—all 31 state governments have environmental laws, although environmentalists point out that many states failed to update their laws after the federal government revised and strengthened environmental laws in 1996. But the Mexican Congress failed to approve fiscal reforms that would provide more funding to regional governments in 2001, and capacity building efforts are mostly in pilot program phases across Mexico.

In 1999, Semarnap adopted a new strategy for decentralizing environmental management functions and devised new financing mechanisms for environmental investments at the state level. These strategies, based on cost recovery for environmental services and the polluter-pays principle, have not yet been implemented, however. Decentralization still relies heavily on direct federal transfers, with only minimal contributions from subnational governments, utilities, and service users. Many of these transfers are more responsive to emergencies and less so to clear financial policies designed to stimulate reform, improve efficiency, or make investments. As a result, state and municipal governments have little incentive to generate new sources of revenue, to collect fees, and to operate more efficiently, because services are not linked to performance and governments have little control over how they spend their resources.[38]

Without control over their budgets and the ability to raise funds through bond offerings, taxation, and other revenue-enhancing measures, Mexican states have not enjoyed the kind of decentralization that would lead to sound environmental management practices. As in other Latin American countries, the municipal governments of Mexico traditionally undertook most of their borrowing from central-government credit institutions or central banking facilities, thereby reinforcing centralization. The primary example of this arrangement was the *Solidaridad* community investment program initiated by the Salinas administration, which funded community infrastructure projects while solidifying support for the ruling Institutional Revolutionary Party.

Some of the infrastructure investment initiatives under the Salinas administration actually acted as a counterforce to decentralization. The Salinas administration insisted on the creation of new institutions to link community investment and decisionmaking more directly to the central government.[39] Agreements were established between federal and subnational governments that covered investment priorities and allocation of service functions, as well as the amounts and forms of intergovernmental aid. Each year, federal, state, and, to some extent, municipal governments, were forced to generate these investment and financing priorities. In these transactions, the federal government acted as the senior partner and controlled subnational spending priorities.

In addition to insufficient tax revenues, local and state governments lack experience in designing and financing major infrastructure projects. For this reason, in Mexico's northern border region, the binational Border Environment Cooperation Commission has implemented several programs that provide technical assistance to local governments. In 1994, Mexico began planning decentralization programs in 10 border cities under the 1992 U.S.-Mexican border environmental plan, and that plan eventually expanded to decentralization to four states.

Mexico's decentralization process experienced a substantial setback with the devaluation of the peso in 1994, which affected all 31 Mexican states. In 1996, the states relied on the federal government for about 80 percent of their funds, and the peso crisis forced reductions in state budgets by an average of about 14 percent.[40] The peso devaluation created other setbacks for decentralizing environmental management. In 1993, Mexico signed an environmental agreement with the World Bank for a spending package of $1.95 billion in U.S. dollars ($918 million in World Bank funds and $1.03 million in Mexican funds) to be used over a period of five to eight years. The agreement involved a series of loans: (1) a loan for general improvement of the environmental infrastructure in the northern border region, (2) one for water treatment and supply throughout Mexico, and (3) one for solid waste projects. In 1995, Mexican and World Bank officials renegotiated the loan amount to reduce the scope of the environmental infrastructure program.[41]

Despite the setback, Mexico did use World Bank financing to strengthen the capacity of several state governments to implement their own environmental programs. In 1991, Mexico's National Ecology Institute began a decentralization and capacity building program with World Bank funding and, in 1993, initiated pilot projects in Tamaulipas and Jalisco; the experiment was expanded to Aguascalientes and San Luis Potosi in 1994. The program consisted of financial and technical support, primarily for training of state environmental specialists, for purchase of laboratory equipment, and for technology transfers to the state.

Although Mexico was unable to fully implement planned decentralization projects in 1994, in 1999 the World Bank approved a $606 million adjustment loan to help Mexico decentralize several different kinds of services and transfer them to state and municipal governments.[42] The thrust of these decentralization projects was in the areas of health and education services. The loan aims to provide regional financing while the federal government implements reforms, including borrowing and debt management reforms for subnational governments, improved administration of public finances, and better coordination among different levels of government.

MONITORING AND ANALYSIS OF ENVIRONMENTAL DATA

The success of an environmental program depends on a government's ability to understand environmental conditions, the rate of change in those conditions, and the factors causing environmental stress. These linkages cannot be understood without the capacity to collect, monitor, and analyze data on environmental conditions and stress factors. After data are collected and analyzed, the information is used to devise management programs and to track the success of those programs through performance measurements. It is at this crucial stage of institutional development—the ability to monitor, collect, and analyze data—that Mexico's environmental management often falters. Mexico is limited in its capacity to collect data on ambient environmental quality and industrial emissions data across most media. State and local governments, which often do not have standardized procedures for monitoring or collecting data for the federal government, also impede the federal government's management efforts.

Many examples exist of the limitations posed by inadequate data collection. In Mexico's case, techniques to collect historical data have resulted in lack of both quality and consistency. One example involves data on water quality, an issue of crucial concern to the Mexican government. Mexico cataloged water quality by river and aquifer throughout much of the 1990s, but lacked monitoring data for various streams in various years, and had little data on the quality of underground water. In particular, stream-monitoring data for the year 1995 was missing in several cases, possibly because of the severe economic crisis and funding cutbacks that the federal government had experienced that year.[43]

The quality of the data collected also hampers at least the public understanding of specific pollution problems in individual Mexican states and localities. In 1998, for example, Semarnap offered the public a breakdown of water quality by major river. But the amount of information offered was limited, possibly because of deficiencies in data reporting and data assimilation. Thus, the public could note that an entire river appeared, on average, to be contaminated, or that the water quality of river systems in an entire Mexican state appeared, on average, to be acceptable. What the public could not do is identify a database that depicted water quality by specific stream segment or by specific pollutants. This is a task easily undertaken in many industrialized countries, where such information is used both by the government for issuing effluent discharge permits and for enforcing regulations and by local communities that are actively involved in land use planning decisions.

International Inventories

On the international level, Mexico is limited in its ability to participate in a pollution registry or emissions inventory with Canada and the United States. This situation restricts the CEC's ability to implement and monitor trilateral agreements on long-range pollutants or to provide a foundation of data that can be used to assess the environmental stresses on ecosystems.

For a number of years, Canada and the United States have had in place inventories of the largest sources of industrial emissions. In the United States, this is done through the Toxic Release Inventory; in Canada, through the National Pollutant Release Inventory. These emissions inventories encompass most types of emissions—from air, water, and underground sources. The inventories are used as a way to track emissions trends, as a basis for adopting new environmental regulations, as a planning tool in siting new industry facilities, and as a method of providing pollution information to interested citizens.

The U.S. inventory tracks more types of chemicals—a little more than 600, compared to Canada's 200 or fewer. But by far most of the Canadian chemicals that are tracked utilize common reporting requirements that the U.S. inventory system uses, making joint analysis of long-range pollutants possible. The CEC periodically takes the emissions inventory data from both countries and publishes them in its report, *Taking Stock*, which provides an overview of pollution by each state and province. The report examines at a continental level industrial pollution sent directly into the air, land, and water or sent off-site for treatment or disposal (mostly in landfills).

Under the administration of President Ernesto Zedillo, nongovernmental organizations accused the Mexican president of delaying the adoption of a pollutant inventory plan.[44] However, the environmental ministry defended the administration. Adrián Fernández, then head of environmental information for the environmental ministry, responded that it took the United States 15 years to develop its toxic release inventory regulations, and that Mexico was attempting to implement the inventory plan in 4 or 5 years. He cautioned that, after the government implemented a pollutant registry, it might be some time before federal agencies made the records public, because Mexican industries lacked experience in accurately reporting emissions information.

Canadian and U.S. government officials and representatives of nongovernmental organizations strongly support the creation of environmental databases. Through the CEC these groups have urged Mexico to duplicate these efforts. In June 2001, the Fox administration promised to work with the CEC to adopt an emissions release and pollution transfer registry and make the results of that registry public within two to four years.[45] Completion of this project, which is now in the pilot phase, will allow Mexico to participate in the CEC's trilateral North American Pollutant Release and Transfer Registry. In Mexico, the newly designed—but not yet implemented—system is called the *Registro de Emisiones y Transferencia de Contaminantes*, and it will be similar to the Canadian and U.S. systems. In this endeavor, Mexico is getting assistance not only from the CEC but also from the Organization for Economic Cooperation and Development and the United Nations Institute of Technology and Research, which facilitated a process leading to an emissions inventory system for Mexico that is similar to the U.S. Toxic Release Inventory.

An emissions inventory can assist Mexico in dealing with some of its most chronic contamination problems, including air pollution. Although the government now has an extensive monitoring system in the Valley of Mexico, which includes Mexico City, the monitoring data for mobile sources of pollution are limited, and it is the vehicles that circulate throughout the city that contribute most of the air pollution. Vehicular pollution contributes almost all the carbon monoxide emissions in the Valley of Mexico, more than 75 percent of nitrous oxide emissions, 35 percent of volatile organic compounds, 24 percent of sulfur dioxide, and 41 percent of fine particulate matter.[46] The number of private vehicles in the metropolitan region is growing by about 6 percent annually, but the federal government, because of insufficient data on these vehicles, cannot predict their future contribution to pollution or determine how best to control the problem.

Ability to Conduct Laboratory Analysis

A nation's pollutant release registry is a catalogue of pollution effects by region and industry, which can be used for planning and impact analysis. The registry relies, as do all planning and impact analyses, on a continuous stream of baseline data for monitoring the effects of pollution. Effective compliance with emissions standards also depends on a steady flow of scientific data, many of which can be provided or confirmed only through laboratory analysis. Historically, the number and quality of Mexican environmental laboratories have been limited, and this in turn limits the federal government's ability to monitor environmental stresses and to undertake impact assessments.

In 1992, a World Bank study noted that Mexico had few environmental laboratories and that most operated "in precarious condition," with inadequate space, old equipment, and insufficiently trained technical and support personnel.[47] State-level laboratories conducted basic analyses of water quality. Existing regional laboratories can carry out slightly more complex analyses of air, water, soil, and solid wastes. In 1992, the central laboratory in Mexico City was the only one able to carry out complex analyses, and that facility provided technical support to the entire system.

As part of its plan to transfer routine monitoring and enforcement functions to state governments, in the early 1990s, the federal government planned to consolidate and strengthen its central and regional

Table 6.8
Mexico's Environmental Laboratories, 1986–2000

Year	Laboratories
1986	11 regional, 21 state-level
1992	1 central, 10 regional, 21 older state-level*
2000	1 central, 3 modern regional

*In environmental publications, Mexican officials vowed to close the older, deteriorating state-level facilities and to build modern ones.

Sources: Compiled by author from data available in Sedue, "Aspects of Mexico's Environmental Policy"; Sedue, *Informe de Labores, 1986–1987*; Sedesol, Instituto Nacional de Ecología, *México: Informe de la Situación General, 1993–1994*; and Giugale et al., eds., *Mexico: A Comprehensive Development Agenda*.

laboratories but to phase out its facilities at the state level. (See table 6.8.) The phaseout of state-level laboratories was to work in tandem with the development and certification of state-sponsored laboratories. The federal government also wanted to promote the development of private-sector laboratories.

With World Bank money, the state of Tamaulipas constructed a modern environmental laboratory for testing both air and water emissions outside Ciudad Victoria. The environmental laboratory, which became operational in 1993, is one of a very few such facilities in Mexico and has the potential to decrease the state's reliance on the federal government for the information and documentation necessary to carry out environmental regulatory actions against the private sector.

PUBLIC PARTICIPATION IN ENVIRONMENTAL POLICYMAKING

Environmental consciousness is the key to the development of either national or North American environmental policy. Without some measure of public consensus on the need for environmental protection, governments lack the political support to implement sound management principles. Prodded by the CEC and other international institutions, Mexico has used public participation in environmental decisionmaking and monitoring as one means of extending its recent democratic experience.

In 1994, Semarnap deepened its relationship with the public by establishing a series of committees—including those concerned with water, forestry, fisheries, environmental regulation, and development—to solicit public input and to educate the public on Semarnap's environmental management goals. In addition to local, state, and national officials, the committees consisted of representatives from industry, academia, and environmental organizations. Over the course of the Zedillo administration, the number and type of public consulting committees increased.

The 1996 reforms to Mexican environmental law strengthened public participation by establishing a right to environmental information on proposed development projects.[48] Indeed, some key Semarnap officials consider this to be the Zedillo administration's most important environmental achievement. One Semarnap official reflected on the fact that, a decade earlier the Mexican people had had no public notification about the potential environmental impacts of development projects.

The emphasis on public access to information continued in the early days of the Fox administration. After his appointment as environmental minister in December 2000, Victor Lichtinger created a new office for public participation and transparency in government operations, which is headed by a well-known environmentalist and former head of the CEC's Joint Public Advisory Committee.

In its efforts to increase public participation and publicly available information on the environment, the Mexican government and certain high-profile Mexican environmental organizations received support from the CEC and other international bodies, such as the OECD. Recognizing the global importance of public participation, most of the CEC's activities include a public component, and the environmental accord that created the CEC has a number of provisions guaranteeing input into almost every aspect of the CEC's work. On numerous occasions, the CEC itself has emphasized the importance of public participation through a series of resolutions and statements made by its council, which consists of the three North American environmental ministers.

CEC support—both through its council and its work program for public participation in environmental decisionmaking—has worked to the advantage of Mexican nongovernmental organizations, which were not as politically strong or as well funded as U.S. and Canadian groups at the time that NAFTA was signed. The Mexican government's environmental officials also support these efforts, because the affected ministry often relies on the rising political strength of the country's environmentalists to support efforts to implement changes in environmental policy in the face of resistance from other government agencies.

Article 14 of the North American Agreement on Environmental Cooperation created a mechanism for citizens to file complaints by which complainants can assert that one of the NAFTA governments is failing to effectively enforce its environmental laws. The CEC's secretariat is charged with investigating these complaints if they meet the appropriate criteria. Under certain circumstances, the environmental ministers of the three countries that make up the CEC can instruct its secretariat to make a public factual record of its investigation under Article 15 of the environmental agreement. The threat of a factual record has proved to be a powerful tool both for embarrassing a national government into changing its environmental policies and for strengthening the role of environmental organizations in environmental policymaking. The possibility of a public record also has galvanized the Mexican government into making more of its development plans public.

Under its legal mandate, the CEC also has a variety of citizens' advisory committees and makes an attempt to draw citizen stakeholders into the many work projects that the secretariat annually conducts. But one of the CEC's most important roles in strengthening public participation is its growing role as a clearinghouse of environmental information. In addition to publishing the *Taking Stock* reports and other special data reports, the CEC has established the North American Biodiversity Information Network, which links databases from many institutions on migratory species and is establishing a database on "green" production and another on emerging environmental trends in North America.

SUMMARY

Mexico has substantially strengthened its environmental regulatory regime throughout the 1990s, has very specific plans to reinforce its ability to collect and analyze environmental data and provide new revenue streams based on the polluter-pays principle, and has taken some preliminary steps to monitor industries more closely. Nevertheless, implementation of many federal plans, such as the use of new economic instruments to provide environmental funding, hinges on needed fiscal reforms that have not been implemented.

Notes

[1] World Bank, Country Operations I and Environment Division, Country Department II, Latin America and the Caribbean Region, "Staff Appraisal Report: Mexico Environmental Project," Report no. 10005-ME, Washington, D.C., March 9, 1992, p. 7.

[2] Ibid., p. 8.

[3] Ministry of Urban Development and Ecology (Sedue), "Mexico: Environmental Issues," Fact sheet, Embassy of Mexico, Washington, D.C., September 1992, pp. 14–17.

[4] Ibid.

[5] Ministry of the Environment, Natural Resources and Fisheries (Semarnap), *Mexico: Policies to Promote Sustainable Development* (Mexico City, April 2000), p. 75.

[6] Servicio Universal de Noticias, "Nueva Política Ambiental," Mexico City, June 4, 2001, Reuters Business Briefing Archives, www.briefing.reuters.com (June 18, 2001).

[7] John Authers and Sara Silver, "Trying Times as Mexicans Prepare for an Austere Budget: The Treasury Secretary's Tight Fiscal Policy is Upsetting the Governors," *Financial Times*, October 16, 2002, The Americas section, p. 6.

[8] World Bank, "Staff Appraisal Report, Mexico Environmental Project," p. 9.

[9] Elisabeth Malkin, "Mexico: Uphill Battle," Natural Resources Council Report, Summer 2000, Reuters Business Briefing, www.breifing.reuters.com (July 10, 2001).

[10] Sedue, "Mexico: Environmental Issues," pp. 3–4.

[11] Secretaría de Medio Ambiente, Recursos Naturales y Pesca, Procuraduría Federal de Protección al Ambiente, *Informe Trianual, 1995–1997*, 2nd ed. (Mexico City, 1998), p. 37.

[12] Ibid.

[13] Secretaría de Desarrollo Social, Instituto Nacional de Ecología, *México: Informe de la Situación General en Materia de Equilibrio Ecológico y Protección al Ambiente, 1993–1994* (Mexico City, April 1994), p. 280.

[14] Instituto Nacional de Estadística, Geografía e Informática (INEGI), *Estadísticas de Medio Ambiente, México: Informe de la Situación General en Materia de Equilibrio Ecológico y Protección al Ambiente,* vol. 1: *1997–1998*, published in conjunction with Secretaría de Medio Ambiente, Recursos Naturales y Pesca, Instituto Nacional de Ecología (Mexico City, 1999), p. 607.

[15] Semarnap, *Mexico: Policies to Promote Sustainable Development.*

[16] Malkin, "Mexico: Uphill Battle."

[17] Author's telephone interviews with several environmental attorneys in Mexico City, November 1–December 15, 2001.

[18] Malkin, "Mexico: Uphill Battle."

[19] Semarnap, *Informe Trianual, 1995–1997*, p. 154.

[20] Ibid.

[21] Sedesol, *México: Informe de la Situación General, 1993–1994*, p. 281.

[22] The Lexington Group, "Industrial Environmental Management in Mexico: Results of a Survey," Report of a project sponsored by the Japanese government, The World Bank, and Mexico's National Ecology Institute, 1997. See also Marcelo M. Giugale, Olivier Lafourcade, and Vinh H. Nguyen, eds., *Mexico: A Comprehensive Development Agenda for the New Era* (Washington, D.C.: International Bank for Reconstruction and Development, World Bank, 2001).

[23] INEGI, *Informe de la Situación General, 1997–1998*, p. 602.

[24] Semarnap, *Mexico: Policies to Promote Sustainable Development.*

[25] Author's interview with Profepa officials, Mexico City, November 10, 2000.

[26] Sedesol, *México: Informe de la Situación General, 1993–1994*, p. 148.

[27] Ibid., p. 179.

[28] Organization for Economic Cooperation and Development, *Environmental Performance Reviews: Mexico* (Paris, 1998), p. 141.

[29] Richard Huber, Jack Ruitenbeek, and Ronaldo Serôa da Motta, *Market-Based Instruments for Environmental Policymaking in Latin America and the*

Caribbean: Lessons from Eleven Countries (Washington, D.C.: World Bank, 1997).

[30] Ibid.

[31] One example is the statement issued by the three chairs of the Hemispheric Trade and Sustainability Symposium, organized jointly by the International Institute for Sustainable Development and the World Conservation Union, in collaboration with the United Nations Environmental Program, Regional Office for Latin America. The chairs, Pierre Marc Johnson, Enrique Leff, and David Runnalls, called for a sustainability assessment in a statement, "The FTAA and Hemispheric Integration: Building a Triple-Win Strategy for Trade and Sustainability in the Hemisphere," Quebec City, April 18, 2001.

[32] Ministry of Urban Development and Ecology (Sedue), "Aspects of Mexico's Environmental Policy and the Environmental Situation in Mexico," Mexico City, April 1991.

[33] Sedesol, *México: Informe de la Situación General, 1993–1994,* p. 266.

[34] Ibid., p. 264.

[35] Miguel Pérez and Fabián Muñoz, "Inicia Federalismo en Guanajuato: El 'Estado Piloto' para la Descentralización, Declara Zedillo, Revisarán Funciones de Secretarías de Estado en la Entidad," *Reforma,* July 1, 1995.

[36] Secretaría de Desarrollo Social, "Protección del Medio Ambiente, Acciones" Mexico City, June 5, 1993.

[37] Sedesol, *México: Informe de la Situación General, 1993–1994,* p. 40.

[38] Giugale et al., eds., *Mexico: A Comprehensive Development Agenda,* p. 629.

[39] Tim Campbell, George Peterson, and Jose Brakarz, "Decentralization to Local Government in Latin American Countries: National Strategies and Local Response in Planning, Spending and Management," Regional Sector Study of Decentralization in Latin American Countries, Final Report, World Bank, Washington, D.C., 1995.

[40] Anthony DePalma, "States in Mexico Trying to Avoid Bankruptcy," *New York Times,* national edition, May 10, 1995.

[41] Author's telephone interview with Adrian de Mayo, World Bank, Latin America Department. II, Washington, D.C., July 31, 1995.

[42] World Bank, "World Bank Approves $606 Million to Support Fiscal Decentralization in Mexico," Press release no. 2000/143/LAC, December 15, 1999; available at www.worldbank.org or at www.shcp.gov.mx/ieo/n_docs11. html (June 21, 2001).

[43] INEGI, *México: Informe de la Situación General, 1997–1998.*

[44] Bureau of National Affairs, "U.S., Canada Agree to Set Emission Limits on Regional Sources to Curb Ozone Transport," *International Environment Reporter* 23, no. 5 (March 1, 2000): 194.

[45] Victor Lichtinger, "Informe de Labores del Primer Semestre de Gobierno, Dic. 2000–Mayo 2001," Comunicación Social, Semarnat, Mexico City, June 2001; available from www.semarnat.gob.mx (June 17, 2001).

[46] Mario J. Molina, "Proyecto para el Diseño de una Estrategia Integral de Gestión de la Calidad del Aire en el Valle de Mexico, 2001–2010," Presentation on behalf of the Massachusetts Institute of Technology, Integrated Program on Urban, Regional, and Global Contamination, Mexico City, November 6, 2000.

[47] World Bank, Country Operations I and Environment Division, Country Department II, Latin American and the Caribbean Regional Office, "Staff Appraisal Report, Mexico, Northern Border Environment Project," Report no. 12603-ME, Washington, D.C., May 16, 1994.

[48] Semarnap, *Mexico: Policies to Promote Sustainable Development*, p. 329.

CHAPTER SEVEN

DETERIORATION OF NATURAL RESOURCES AND REMEDIATION EFFORTS

THE ABILITY TO MANAGE POLLUTION AND NATURAL RESOURCES depends not only on the improvement of institutions and management programs but also on the rate at which natural resources deteriorate, a government's ability to effectively use the management tools it has adopted to reduce pollution, and the sheer magnitude of the environmental and economic obstacles that a society faces. This chapter examines the level and rate of the deterioration of Mexico's natural resources and the evolution of resource management across three environmental media: water, land (and forests), and air. Two additional sections discuss the challenge the Mexican government faces in handling municipal, industrial, and toxic wastes.

Progress in dealing with the deterioration of natural resources and pollution reduction is categorized by the following measures:

- gathering and monitoring data,
- recognizing the problem and passing legislative reforms to address the issue,
- planning environmental protection and remediation programs to address the problem, and
- implementing programs that deal with the problem effectively.

This chapter also includes a discussion of institutional and financial obstacles to implementing the government's goals. The financial obstacles are a reflection not only of national fiscal management policies but also of the severity of the natural resource challenges Mexico faces.

WATER RESOURCES

The Challenge

Mexico is a country with scarce water resources, which are also severely polluted and inefficiently used. Data gathered by the Organization for Economic Cooperation and Development (OECD) indicate that several thousand Mexicans die each year from the effects of poor water quality. The pollution and inefficient use of water reflect decades of weak environmental management and little investment in urban infrastructure. Today, the lack of potable water in Mexico threatens not only future economic development but also the supply of clean water needed for basic human consumption. In 2001, Mexico's Secretary of the Environment Victor Lichtinger told the *New York Times* that "there is no place in this country, with the exception of maybe one or two cities, like Monterrey, where you can drink the water without worrying you're going to get sick."[1]

One of Mexico's greatest challenges in maintaining a clean water supply is the failure to adequately manage municipal and agricultural wastewater and agricultural runoff. Poor conveyance infrastructure also inhibits the government's stated goal of water conservation. About 28 percent of Mexico's total wastewater is generated in urban areas, and the federal government's statistics show that only 22 percent of all municipal wastewater was treated in 1999.[2] In 1977, World Bank researchers estimated that only 5–10 percent of total effluents were treated.[3] Existing municipal wastewater plants often do not operate because of the lack of funds needed for maintenance. As of July 2001, Mexico's National Water Commission reported that only 186 of 777 plants were in operation.

Agricultural wastewater and runoff, including pesticides and fertilizer residuals, contribute 62 percent of the nation's wastewater. Most untreated wastes flow into the five river basins that are the principal sources of Mexico's supply of surface water.

Mexico City's water conveyance system is in such poor condition that half of the water pumped into the city is lost because of leaks and cracks. The city's aqueducts are so old that some of them date to the time of the Aztec empire five centuries ago.

In addition to water pollution, the growing shortage of water has alarmed President Fox. In interviews with journalists during the first year of his administration, Fox called the water problem a national security issue. About 12 million out of 100 million Mexicans have no potable water supply, he said. Those who can afford to do so have water trucked into rural areas, but this is a very expensive measure. Along with poor water delivery systems—a problem that has plagued Mexico for many decades—an eight-year drought has reduced the supply of water in northern and central Mexico.

The inefficiency of the infrastructure for agricultural irrigation causes water losses of 45–60 percent of flow volumes, according to Mexican and World Bank analyses. Thus, although the value of agricultural production has remained steady for two decades, the costs of production are rising, and the continuing use of dwindling water supplies is not sustainable.

Water Shortage

In spring 2001, Mexico's National Water Commission reported that the country's per capita potable water supply has dropped by 60 percent over the past 50 years, as a growing population depletes existing resources. The shortage is expected to increase in the next decade.[4]

Part of Mexico's water shortage in urban areas reflects geographic realities—uneven and poorly distributed rainfall patterns. Only about 20 percent of all rainfall occurs in the populated areas of central and northern Mexico, where 77 percent of the nation's gross domestic product is produced. Most of the rain falls in less-populated regions with little economic or agricultural development. And, although Mexico has 316 river basins, only about 15 percent of surface water is above an elevation of 500 meters, where about 75 percent of the Mexican population lives and where 80 percent of industrial plants are located.[5] Thus, a significant portion of Mexico's energy is used for pumping water to population and industry centers.

Drought also plays a role in the unsustainable use of aquifers in northern and central Mexico's regions of intense agricultural production or population density. Mexico has 649 aquifers and relies heavily on underground water supplies in its northern states, where rainfall is scarce. However, these resources are being depleted as well. As early as 1992, a World Bank study warned that 80 major aquifers in Mexico were overexploited and that irrigated agriculture in high-elevation, arid, and semiarid regions was primarily responsible for inefficient water use.[6] In 1999, the *Secretaría de Medio Ambiente, Recursos Naturales y Pesca* (Semarnap) reported that water extraction from 96 aquifers exceeded the natural recharge rate and that 18 aquifers were experiencing intrusion from salt water.[7]

Another part of Mexico's water shortage reflects inefficient use in agricultural production. As shown in table 7.1, across Mexico, agribusinesses, mining firms, and cattle ranchers consume 83 percent of the nation's water, according to 2000 estimates. As with the water conveyance systems for large urban areas, the agricultural system is plagued with so many leaks that about half the water volume in those areas is lost.

Water Pollution

Aside from problems of poor spatial distribution, Mexico's existing surface and underground water sources face increasing rates of contamination from poor land use practices and poor handling of municipal and industrial wastes. Lack of basic infrastructure is the key to the pollution problem. Mexican cities were established or expanded without the construction of basic infrastructure services, such as sewerage systems, and conflicts between the federal and local governments over provision of infrastructure services have limited the modernization of most cities.

The infrastructure deficit is evident on the municipal level. Little municipal wastewater is treated, and untreated wastes flow into Mexico's principal river basins. Semarnap reported that about 22 percent of municipal wastewater received treatment in 1999; this figure rose to 24 percent in 2000. In 1997, however, World Bank researchers reported that only about 5–10 percent of total effluents were being treated.[8]

Much of Mexico's polluted surface water flows into the nation's five principal river basins, and water quality in those basins has been falling steadily since the 1980s. According to Mexico's own water

Table 7.1
Mexico's Water Use, 1990–2000

Year	Percent of Population without Potable Water	Percent of Population without Access to Sewage System	Percent Used for Agriculture
1990	22.3	39.1	No data
1991	21.0	37.5	No data
1992	19.6	36.2	85.0
1993	18.7	35.4	No data
1994	17.8	34.3	No data
1995	15.8	27.9	No data
1996	15.1	27.6	No data
1997	14.1	27.6	No data
1998	13.6	27.5	76.0
2000	12.0	24.0	83.0

Sources: Compiled by author from data available in Secretaría de Desarrollo Social (Sedesol), "Protección del Medio Ambiente, Acciones," Mexico City, June 5, 1993; Ministry of Urban Development and Ecology "Aspects of Mexico's Environmental Policy and the Environmental Situation in Mexico," Mexico City, April 1991; Sedesol, Instituto Nacional de Ecología, *México, Informe de la Situación General en Materia de Equilibrio Ecológico y Protección al Ambiente, 1993–1994* (Mexico City, 1995); and Marcelo M. Giugale, Olivier Lafourcade, and Vinh H. Nguyen, eds., *Mexico: A Comprehensive Development Agenda for the New Era* (Washington, D.C.: International Bank for Reconstruction and Development, World Bank, 2001).

quality index, the quality of the water in the five most contaminated river basins fell 5.3 percent from 1989 to 1991. In 1994, the federal government determined that four rivers—the Panuco, Lerma, San Juan, and Balsas—received 50 percent of all wastewater, including untreated municipal wastewater.[9] Just 20 of the nation's river basins absorbed a total of 89 percent of the pollution.

Table 7.2
Surface Water Contamination, 2001

Percent	Level of Contamination
10.3	Excessively contaminated
6.6	Strongly contaminated
58.4	Contaminated
17.6	Lightly contaminated
6.9	Acceptable
0.2	Excellent

Source: Compiled by author from information found in Daniel Millan, "Si el Rio Suena Contaminacion Lleva, Alertan Sobre Problema de Salud Pública," *Reforma*, April 2, 2001.

By 2001, environmental ministry officials were reviewing results of a new study showing that 93 percent of all Mexican rivers and streams were polluted.[10] (Table 7.2 provides a breakdown of the contamination levels.) When groundwater contamination is included, 73 percent of Mexico's water supply is considered polluted. In contrast, in June 1998, the U.S. Environmental Protection Agency (EPA) reported that about 40 percent of U.S. waters surveyed were too polluted for basic uses and announced cleanup actions.[11]

Evolution of Resource Management

In 1974, Mexico established a national water-monitoring system to gather baseline data on levels of contamination in principal water bodies. As of 1994, that system included 793 monitoring points covering 196 rivers, underground water supplies, 42 dams, 25 drainage systems, 13 canals, 12 coastal zones, 5 estuaries, 22 lakes and lagunas, 7 creeks, and 7 deep rock pools. However, that same year, the Mexican government conceded that its monitoring system was still not extensive enough to provide enough data to quantify or analyze certain types of water pollution, such as underground water pollution from inadequate disposal of garbage, pollution from certain types of agrochemicals, erosion, acid runoff from mining operations, and deposits from certain types of air contaminates in bodies of water.

Mexico's 1982 economic crisis had an adverse impact on water conservation, because it strongly affected irrigation infrastructure. Funds were simply not available for modernizing or even maintaining this system; as a result, over the years, Mexico's irrigation infrastructure has become neglected and is now substandard.

Mexico has revised its water laws and management practices over the past decade, but often the regulations are not enforced at the municipal level. In 1989, the National Water Commission was established as a semiautonomous agency within Semarnap. The commission had full authority over most water management issues, including inspection as well as enforcement of federal water laws and associated regulations. Gradually, however, over the next decade, regional governments have begun to take over some of the commission's tasks, such as implementing clean water mandates. Even before the commission was created, municipalities had responsibility for drinking water and sewerage services. Because few cities could effectively provide these services, in the late 1990s, water utilities were established and were funded partly or wholly with local or state funds.

President Salinas de Gortari focused on providing potable water in 1991. In creating a Clean Water Program, he tried to force municipal governments and industries to comply with treatment regulations. The program had some beneficial effects. At the time the law was implemented, only 250 Mexican municipal governments were disinfecting their municipal water supplies, but by 1994, that number had increased to 14,690.[12] Because many other cities failed to comply, in 1997 the federal government set a deadline of January 1, 2000, for cities to start treating their water. Again, many cities failed to comply, including Mexico City.[13]

Pollution fees for discharges into public waters also were established in 1991, but even today the revenue does not cover operating costs for the services provided, and only a part of the water that is used is subject these charges.[14] The goal of this policy was to reduce the volume of wastewater and to induce companies to invest in improving water quality. Enforcement of the fees has always been inconsistent, however, and in June 2001, Cristóbal Jaime, president of the National Water Commission, said that nonpayment of water user fees to state and local governments had resulted in $6.81 billion in outstanding debts for water services.[15]

The 1992 Law on National Waters, Mexico's first general water law, aimed for additional conservation and increased regulation. The law established three instruments for water management: concessions to take water, permits to discharge effluents into national waters, and a public registry of water rights. The law also paved the way for a water market by establishing conditions under which concessions and permits could be transferred to other users. A separate Mexican law, the Federal Law on Water Excise Taxes, established water as an economic asset as well as the polluter-pays principle. As with the collection of water user fees, however, the provisions for water users to hold concessions to take water have never been fully enforced. The OECD's 1998 environmental performance review of Mexico stated that more than 300,000 water users were required to hold these concessions or to apply for permits to discharge effluents. Many users had failed to do so, however, and this resulted in a considerable loss of both revenue and water management authority.

The 1992 water law called for a new, comprehensive national water program. As a partial response, in 1994, the federal government implemented regulations establishing regional master management plans for river basins and aquifers, improvements to groundwater, and monitoring of surface water. The management plans also called for additional modeling and assessment of water quality, improvements to the operation of hydraulic infrastructure, and enhancements to meteorological services.[16] Nevertheless, by 1997, Mexico still was attempting to establish methodologies and was undertaking pilot projects for water conservation and sustainable agricultural practices in several regions, including one in the state of Guanajuato.

Striving for Sustainability

The severity of Mexico's water crisis implies a need for massive expenditures not only for mitigating contamination but also for extending potable water to rural communities, for providing sewage treatment to urban areas that currently lack such services, and for keeping up with growing demand for urban water. Although a number of cities have wastewater treatment systems, many are not operational because cities do not have the funding to maintain them. In 2001, the National Water Commission estimated that the cost of putting a halt to water contamination and providing enough water treatment to keep pace with people's needs would be at least $30 billion over the next decade.[17] As a way of gauging the magnitude of the investment, it is useful to look at the challenges faced by the United States. In June 1998, the EPA estimated that $139.5 billion was needed across the United States to construct or improve wastewater treatment facilities in order to correct water quality and address public health problems.[18]

To provide the funding required to clean up the water supply and to modernize the infrastructure, Mexico needs substantial fiscal reforms that will raise revenue and generate a culture of water conservation. Even though Mexico's agribusinesses use an estimated 76 percent of Mexico's water supply, this sector is exempt from water use fees. Victor Lichtinger believes that the Fox administration's most important fiscal reform relating to the environment would be to force agribusinesses to pay for their water and to use revenues from those fees to modernize Mexico's water and wastewater treatment systems. President Fox's fiscal reform package, submitted to the Mexican Congress in spring 2001, contained such a measure, but Congress ultimately rejected much of his proposed reform. World Bank researchers also have suggested that the Mexican government should revise water use fees for public utilities and that the federal government should eliminate the electricity subsidy for agriculture, a utility that is heavily used by irrigators.

However, the Fox administration is likely to face significant political obstacles both in instituting such fees and in eliminating agricultural subsidies. Over the past 20 years, the portion of Mexico's agricultural production that came from irrigated methods rose from 45 percent to 55 percent of total production value. Because irrigated agriculture provides 70 percent of agricultural exports, this sector contributes substantially to Mexico's trade balance; therefore, it is important for Mexico to keep up productivity in this sector.

Mexico also will need to strengthen the monitoring of water quality and management of aquifers as quickly as possible. Water engineers maintain that pollution of groundwater is reversible only at very high costs, if at all, and has the potential to damage human health and economic development permanently.

Finally, the Mexican government will have to reverse a longstanding culture of nonpayment and failure to enforce payment of existing user fees. The National Water Commission estimates that only 30 percent of water bills are paid, even though fees are set so low that they represent a heavy subsidy. As a result, most city councils and state governments do not collect the funds they need to cover their own infrastructure operating expenses.

LAND AND FORESTS

The Challenge

For Mexico, growing crises in soil degradation and deforestation reflect important examples of the lag time between economic development and the integration of environmental and economic policies. These problems have been evident since the 1940s, and today, the cumulative effects of soil erosion threaten Mexico's biodiversity, its water supply, and its future agricultural productivity. Loss of forests also increases Mexico's contribution to the worldwide total emissions of carbon dioxide, a greenhouse gas. The deterioration of land and forests is so great that the World Bank has predicted that some part of the environmental damage cannot be mitigated.

Deforestation statistics for Mexico vary significantly from one study to another, depending on the methodology used to estimate forest loss. For this reason, tables 7.3 and 7.4 give two measures of forest loss for comparative purposes.[19] Despite differences in

Table 7.3
Variation in Mexico's Forest Cover, 1950–1995
(in millions of hectares)

Period	Variation in Total Forested Area	Total Hectares Lost	Hectares Lost Annually
Original forests to 1950	77.8–98.0	20.2	ND
1950–1970	67.8–77.8	10.0	0.5
1970–1980	60.8–67.8	7.0	0.7
1980–1990	56.8–60.8	4.0	0.4
1990–1995	55.3–56.8	1.5	0.3

Sources: Compiled by author from information available in Secretaría de Agricultura y Recursos Hidráulicos, Subsecretaría Forestal y de Fauna Silvestre, *Inventario Nacional Forestal Periódico, 1992–1994* (Mexico City, 1994); and Secretaría de Medio Ambiente, Recursos Naturales y Pesca (Semarnap), Subsecretaría de Recursos Naturales, "Balance de la Superficie Forestal, 1950–1997," available at www.semarnap.gob.mx (July 4, 2001).
Note: Number includes natural forests and forest plantations.

methodology, however, Mexico's rate of deforestation steadily increased from the 1940s through the 1990s, culminating in high rates between 1970 and 1980—close to the same rate in a 10-year period as in the previous 20-year period. (See table 7.3.) According to one recent estimate, out of a national territory of about 197 million hectares, Mexico lost an average of 615,000 hectares of forests each year from 1980 to 1990—4 percent of deforestation worldwide.[20]

Although the annual rate of deforestation may have decreased over the decade of the 1990s, as the figures in table 7.3 show, by the late 1990s, the cumulative effect of decades of deforestation was clear. Estimates of the loss vary, but all estimates demonstrate considerable decline. In 1998, Semarnap estimated that Mexico had lost almost 74 percent of its forest coverage from 1950 through 1997. OECD estimates, based on Mexican data, are similar. These data show that forests that once covered 75 percent of Mexico's territory now cover only about 25 percent of the national territory.[21]

Table 7.4
Changes in Mexico's Forest Cover, 1950–1997
(in square kilometers)

Forest Area	1950–1969	1970–1979	1980–1989	1990–1994	1993	1994	1995	1996	1997
Initial Area[1]	669,481	587,824	531,404	504,704	496,038	495,367	494,983	494,505	494,026
Deforestation[2]	100,000	70,000	40,000	15,000	2,300	2,019	1,998	1,998	1,998
Recuperation[3]	18,343	13,580	13,300	5,279	1,629	1,635	1,520	1,519	1,719
Natural	12,343	5,580	5,300	2,079	521	520	520	519	519
Artificial[4]	6,000	8,000	8,000	3,200	1,108	1,115	1,000	1,000	1,200
Area at end of period	587,824	531,404	504,704	494,983	495,367	494,983	494,505	494,026	493,747

Source: Compiled by author from information available in Semarnap, Subsecretaría de Recursos Naturales, "Balance de la Superficie Forestal, 1950–1997," www.semarnap.gob.mx (July 4, 2001).

1 The estimate for the forest area from 1950 to 1994 is based on historical deforestation rates, using data from the Strategic Forestry Program of 1997. The figures given for forest coverage after 1994 are based on results from the Mexican National Forestry Inventory.

2 The data for 1995–1997 are estimated using a national average annual deforestation rate of 0.403 percent, which represents an annual loss of 0.403 hectares for every 100 hectares.

3 Natural forest recuperation rate is estimated at 0.105 percent.

4 The average artificial recuperation rate was estimated at 30,000 hectares per year for the period 1950–1969 and at 80,000 hectares per year for the period 1970–1994, taking into account the forest plantations established during the latter period.

Table 7.5
Mexico's Soil Erosion, Selected Years

Year	Percent of Territory Eroded
1945	45
1965	69
1980	80
1986	81-86
1993	85

Sources: Compiled by author from data available in Giugale et al., eds., *Mexico: A Comprehensive Development Agenda*; Semarnap, *La Gestión Ambiental en México* (Mexico City, October 2000); and Organization for Economic Cooperation and Development, *OECD Environmental Data, Compendium 1995* (Paris, 1995).
Note: Methods used to quantify erosion vary over time.

Mexico carried out its most recent forest inventory in 2000, using satellite images that were compared with satellite data from an earlier forest inventory conducted in 1992–1994. Results from the two surveys, combined with other estimates, indicated that primary and secondary forest vegetation had shrunk by 3 million hectares (74.4 million to 71.2 million hectares) in the 17-year period from 1976 to 1993.[22]

The rate of soil erosion in Mexico is as accelerated as the rate of deforestation. Together, man-made and natural phenomena, such as wind erosion, result in an annual loss of nearly 460,000 tons of soil, which washes into oceans and lakes and against dams. As table 7.5 shows, the percentage of land eroded increased dramatically from 1945 to 1980, and the OECD's 1998 environmental review of Mexico stated that, as a result of soil erosion, 60 percent of Mexican territory was seriously affected by desertification.[23] In 1999, a Semarnap report noted that some degree of soil degradation had affected virtually all of Mexico's territory.[24] In 1994, Semarnap estimated that about 154 million hectares—about 78.3 percent of national territory—were subject to some level of erosion and indicated that this was one of the principal causes of desertification. The government estimated that between 74 million and 94 million hectares experienced only light or moderate erosion, but another 60 million to 80 million were severely eroded.

Agricultural Fertility

In about 1980, Mexico's agricultural officials predicted that, without adequate soil and water conservation measures, production of maize, a staple in the Mexican diet, would fall by about 12.5 percent by the year 2000. In reality, the overall value of Mexico's agricultural production has remained nearly constant over the past 20 years, but this has occurred in large measure because a greater percentage of production comes from irrigated production in the semiarid regions of northern Mexico. The shift to irrigated agriculture is not sustainable, because it is sapping a greater portion of Mexico's dwindling water supply. In addition, agricultural productivity is expected to drop—or the cost of it to rise—as a result of soil conditions, which are partially caused by continuing erosion. As of 1994, the *Secretaría de Desarrollo Social* (Sedesol) estimated that only 14 percent of the land available for cultivation was in optimal condition for planting.[25]

In 1996, Mexico characterized the fertility of its agricultural land according to five simple categories that ranged from "very high fertility" to "very low" fertility. More than half of all agricultural land fell into the categories of "very low," "low," or "medium" fertility.[26] Although not a definitive study, the data collected did imply that Mexico could not maintain current levels of agricultural productivity much longer. Again in 2001, Environmental Secretary Victor Lichtinger announced that soil erosion and water shortages were reducing available agricultural land.[27] He said that recent studies showed that about 60 percent of Mexican territory within mountainous regions has some degree of erosion, and that 20 percent is severely eroded. As topsoil at high elevations erodes, the land loses its ability to absorb rainfall; this situation contributes not only to desertification but also to flooding in lower elevations.

Loss of Biodiversity

Mexico has about 10 percent of the world's known species of flora and fauna, up to 50 percent of which is endemic. Changes in land use patterns, particularly in agriculture, threaten many of these species, however. According to OECD statistics, Mexico's use of land for agriculture increased by 40 percent between 1970 and 1990, while deforestation rates remain quite high.[28] A total of 24,000 species of flora and fauna have been identified in Mexico, excluding invertebrates and nonvascular plants. Of these, 315 were at risk of extinction in 1998, another 790 were threatened, and 1,130 were rare in 1998, according to OECD data.

Evolution of Resource Management

Mexico first approved a forest conservation law in 1926,[29] but for the next 65 years little effective action was taken to implement sustainable land management practices. The continuing rate of deforestation, accompanied by the expansion in agriculture and livestock grazing, provides clear evidence of this fact. Until the 1980s, Mexico's policy on the use of forests focused on large-scale timber extraction and processing and provided little support to communal forest owners. These forest owners, whose unsustainable agricultural practices also contribute to deforestation and soil erosion, received more attention after 1980, but agricultural and livestock grazing practices continued to shrink Mexico's forest coverage. Between 1980 and 1990, forest fires, primarily set for agricultural purposes, caused 48.2 percent of the deforestation in temperate forest zones.[30] For other types of forests, 58.1 percent of the destruction came from livestock grazing.

In 1980, the Mexican agricultural secretariat sponsored satellite imagery studies that revealed that soil erosion caused by deforestation was increasing at an alarming rate throughout the country and that much of the damage was irreversible.[31] With increasingly serious signs of deforestation emerging in the 1980s and early 1990s, the Mexican government responded in crisis mode, launching an extensive tree-planting program, in which more than 90 percent of the trees planted did not survive for more than one year. One example of

Table 7.6
Mexico's Reforestation Efforts, Selected Years

Years	Number of Trees Planted	Hectares Covered	Purpose
1986–1987	800,000	890	Reforestation of protected areas
1986–1987	135,000	135	Reduction of soil erosion
1995–1997	810,000,000	313,000	Primarily rural reforestation (77%)
1998–1999	579,000,000	429,000	Primarily rural reforestation

Sources: Compiled by author from information available in Semarnap, Subsecretaría de Recursos Naturales, "Balance de la Superficie Forestal, 1950-1997," www.semarnap.gob.mx (July 4, 2001); Instituto Nacional de Estadística, Geografía e Informática (INEGI), *Estadísticas del Medio Ambiente, México: Informe de la Situación General en Materia de Equilibrio Ecológico y Protección al Ambiente*, vol. 2: *1999*, published in conjunction with Instituto Nacional de Ecología, Semarnap (Mexico City, 2000); and Secretaría de Desarrollo Urbano y Ecología "Ecología: Concertación de Voluntades," Mexico City, 1987.

the government's efforts along these lines is the mobilization of citizens to participate in a 1990 program, called "One Family, One Tree," under which Mexican families planted 1.8 million trees.[32] In 1995, Mexico established the National Reforestation Program (*Pronare*), under which, from 1995 through 1997, 810 million trees were planted on 313,000 hectares—77 percent in rural areas and 23 percent in urban ones.[33] As shown in table 7.6, another 429,000 hectares were reforested with 579 million trees in 1998–1999.

Mexico strengthened its forestry law and related regulations throughout the 1990s. The federal government began the process in 1992 with a modification to Article 27 of the Mexican Constitution, which expanded governmental authority to deal with land use. This step was taken not only to provide a legal basis for land management practices designed to reverse soil erosion but also to provide authority over practices related to desertification.

That same year, Mexico also established a new forestry law emphasizing reforestation and new measures to prevent and mitigate deforestation and to control forest fires. The new law also favored measures aimed at reducing or eliminating subsidies to large-scale

Table 7.7
Expansion of Mexico's Protected Area System

Year	Reserves	Hectares
1992	83	6.16 million
1999	116	12.7 million

Sources: Compiled by author from information available in Semarnap, Subsecretaría de Recursos Naturales, "Balance de la Superficie Forestal, 1950–1997," www.semarnap.gob.mx (July 4, 2001); and INEGI, Semarnap, *México: Informe de la Situación General, 1999.*

timber operations. Regulations under that general law were promulgated in 1994. In 1994, Semarnap also implemented a series of new regulations aimed at mitigating the adverse impacts of industrial forest use on land and bodies of water. However, these legal changes did not stop the devastating forest fires that swept across 500,000 acres of Chiapas in 1998, consuming the area's rain forests.

As part of the national effort to reverse deforestation, in the mid- to late 1990s, Semarnap also focused on expanding Mexico's system of protected natural areas and its management techniques for those areas. (See table 7.7.) Throughout most of modern Mexican history, regulations governing the use of land in protected areas were scarce and almost never enforced. Consequently, unregulated development within the borders of protected areas severely damaged many of them.

In the late 1990s, Semarnap launched a technical assistance program for land use zoning at the local level and in 1997 began a capacity building and technical assistance pilot project for forest communities in Oaxaca. That project brought 165,000 hectares under improved management, established some new conservation areas, and at the same time created some permanent forest-based jobs. Semarnap also equipped 36 reserves with permanent staff, infrastructure, and a management budget. All 36 of these reserves now have management plans that Semarnap officials have approved.[34]

As a result of these measures, by 2000, a total of 66 percent of Mexico's protected system—representing 10,707,246 hectares—was covered by management plans. And although traditionally none of the protected areas were staffed by park personnel, by 2000, 88 percent of the protected areas had some staff presence.[35]

Aside from protecting forests in designated natural areas, the government is still experimenting with institutional structures that will result in better soil and forest management. In 1999, the Mexican government took preliminary steps to forming a new forest management plan: gathering data on land use practices and environmental stresses, compiling lists of scientists and institutions with expertise in soil conservation, collecting other types of information needed to assess the impacts of soil erosion on ecosystems, and attempting to reorient land use regulations to sustainable practices.[36]

The next steps will be political ones. Agricultural land use practices in Mexico are not sustainable, but they do involve additional institutional reforms of well-entrenched agricultural practices that have existed since the end of the Mexican Revolution in 1920. The federal government's goals, therefore, are often frustrated by the inability of rural communities to carry out the management tasks necessary to conserve the fertility of land used for agriculture. As a result, in 1998, Semarnap set out to obtain the participation of these communities in the process of diagnosing local ecosystem stresses, choosing approaches to sustainable agriculture, and preventing and controlling soil degradation.[37]

Clearly, Mexico's ability to inventory its forests and integrate results of those inventories into management plans is improving. When the federal government sponsored satellite imaging of forests on a state-by-state basis in 1980, the resulting inventory was used to create studies of individual states. None of the information in the studies was used for a nationwide assessment.[38] But in 1991–1992, when Mexico again sponsored another forest inventory, more detailed results from satellite imagery were compiled into a nationwide analysis, and the information also was integrated into a national management plan. With the 1991–1992 inventory in hand, the Mexican government had a basis for comparison when it conducted the forest inventory in 2000.

In 2000, Semarnap officials said they had initiated other economic reforms aimed at reversing the development policies of early decades that had contributed substantially to deforestation and soil erosion. Officials said they had eliminated subsidies for cattle grazing in tropical forests, prohibited new commercial agricultural ventures in remaining forest areas, and stopped reforestation efforts for communal farming lands. The government also implemented new legislation and management strategies for overall forestry management: reforestation efforts that once focused primarily on public easement adornments, where only about 6 percent of the seedlings survived, shifted in 1997 to recuperation of ecosystems. Since then, the one-year survival rate for planted trees has grown to 20 percent of all trees planted, Semarnap officials said in November 2000.[39]

Striving for Sustainability

Deforestation rates in Mexico have decreased from the extremely high rates found between 1950 and 1980. With more effective land use practices and continuing reforestation programs, Mexico can slow the rate of forest loss even more. But even at slower rates, the Office of the Federal Attorney General for Environmental Protection (Profepa) has estimated that, in the next 25 years, another 12.5 million hectares of forests will be lost, representing about 22 percent of the Mexico's remaining forests.

Much of the soil erosion, which leads to desertification, is not reversible, nor is the loss of biodiversity. In addition, worsening soil conditions tend to affect remaining forests. Semarnap records show that a portion of Mexico's remaining forests is threatened by disease and invasive plant species.

Mexico will need not only funding but also the political will to solve these problems. The country is unique in that about 80 percent of its forest area is within community boundaries. Since no property rights have been established for these *ejidos* (indigenous communally held farming communities), environmental management practices continue to be limited. Political will also is needed to enforce existing forestry laws. In the tropical forest areas of southern Mexico, illegal extraction of wood continues to be a problem because of insufficient management budgets and not enough personnel for monitoring and managing resources. Mexican planning officials pointed out that what Mexico needs is for conservation to become firmly entrenched as part of the Mexican culture.

URBAN AIR QUALITY

The Challenge

Over the past two decades, Mexico's most formidable challenge related to air quality has been to alleviate the health crisis posed by the poor quality of Mexico City's air. In 1992, this crisis prompted the United Nations to declare Mexico City's air to be the world's most polluted. In 1991, the city's air quality was so poor that it triggered 44 environmental emergencies that necessitated the closure of industries and banned cars from the city's roads for 61 days. In 1992, one air emergency alert paralyzed the city for two weeks.

Mexico City's air quality is improving, but the city's government will continue to bear a significant cost to keep up the improvements over the next decade. Mexico already is using World Bank and Inter-American Development Bank loans to provide cleaner technologies in Mexico City's transportation sector.

Monitoring of air quality is far more limited outside of Mexico City, and environmentalists complain that the government has little idea of the health threats posed by deteriorating air quality in midsized cities. State and municipal authorities and, in some cases, private entities operate most monitoring stations outside Mexico City. The efforts of these local networks vary in the amount of information collected on pollutants and in the degree of local capacity to manage the systems. The federal government has supported the development of a national monitoring network by providing some budget, equipment, and technical assistance, but large gaps remain. The World Bank and the EPA have also supported the development of the national network through financial resources and technical assistance.

The cities where air quality is most likely to change are the largest cities with the greatest number of industries and vehicles. Aside from

Mexico City, these include Guadalajara, Monterrey, and Toluca. Some of the border cities—including Ciudad Juárez, Tijuana, and Mexicali—not quite so large as Mexico's megacities but have substantial amounts of vehicular and industrial emissions. In recent years, the environmental ministry conducted inventories of air emissions in all these cities, to the extent that monitoring data were available. In all, the government recognized one consistent pattern across cities: the transportation sector generated the most serious contamination affecting human health. For the ministry, this finding implied a need to implement nationwide vehicle inspection programs and other regulatory measures to reduce vehicular emissions. The government now is embarking on a second stage of analysis to analyze fine particulate emissions from vehicles, industry, unpaved roads, and deforested areas. The government is also promoting strategies to enforce emissions standards and vehicle inspection programs in cities across the country.

Evolution of Air Quality Management

Semarnap and the government of Mexico City made a concerted effort to improve air quality management in the Valley of Mexico throughout the decade of the 1990s; and since 1993, air emergencies have gradually subsided in Mexico City. However, heat, drought, and forest fires caused particulate matter to reach record levels in 1998. Nevertheless, the number of days that the Valley of Mexico's air quality fell to the point of being declared an "air emergency" by federal criteria decreased from about 55 days in 1991 to fewer than 10 in 1997.[40]

Part of this improvement came as a result of technical assistance from foreign governments. In 1988, the U.S. and Mexican governments formed a binational working group to study air quality; and in 1989 they signed an agreement to work toward improving Mexico City's air management system. Under this agreement, the EPA's Office of Research and Development contributed a monitoring system, personnel training in running the system, and technicians who annually audited the program and calibrated the monitoring equipment. However, as late as 1992, the year Profepa began operations, the newly established office had almost no data on industry emissions with which to do its work.

Many technical studies of the problem of air quality in Mexico City were conducted from the late 1980s through the mid-1990s with technical cooperation of the governments of the United States, Japan, the United Kingdom, and Germany. The United Nations also offered some technical training to Mexico through its Institute for Training and Research. The Japanese government has been particularly active in establishing baseline data on ambient air quality in Mexico City's urban airshed. It was during this period that Mexico established an air quality monitoring system and an ambient air quality index for the city with the help of the Japanese government. The Mexican government also established, and later refined, a contingency system for shutting down industries when temperature inversions cause ambient air quality to deteriorate to dangerous levels.

The 1988 omnibus environmental act provided a framework for air quality management, but it was not until 1993 that Mexico implemented the technical regulations needed for monitoring fixed and mobile sources of air pollution. Today, Mexico's ambient air quality standards are similar to U.S. National Ambient Air Quality Standards, although Mexico's air monitoring network is not well established. It was the 1979 adoption of the National Environmental Policy Act that spurred interest among Mexican officials to improve air quality management and prompted them to begin making numerous trips to the United States for discussions on air quality legislation and implementation in the early 1980s.

Alejandro Encinas, Mexico City's environmental secretary in 2000, said the city's efforts to improve air quality had begun in earnest in 1990, with comprehensive programs directed at transportation, industry, reforestation, and environmental education.[41] Both the Salinas and the Zedillo administrations tightened technical standards for air quality for Mexico City. Under President Salinas, Mexico City's oil refineries and lead foundries were closed as well.

In Mexico City, the levels of lead, carbon monoxide, and sulfur dioxide dropped with the implementation of a comprehensive air quality management program that integrated environmental concerns in the transportation sector. Measures initiated included oxygenation of gasoline to improve combustion; elimination of lead from gasoline; use of catalytic converters; reduction in volatile and toxic chemicals in motor fuels; a vehicle verification program that tests for hydrocarbons, carbon monoxide, ozone, and nitrogen oxides; efforts to install vapor recovery systems in the city's gas stations; and expansion of public transportation. Lead was removed from gasoline in July 1997, and officials of the state-owned oil and gas firm, Pemex, said that the quality of Mexico City's gasoline and diesel fuel is now comparable to that in the United States, except for the amount of sulfur the fuels contain. However, the level of vehicular emissions in Mexico drops more slowly than the U.S. level does, because vehicles tend to be used, on average, for many more years in Mexico than they are in the United States.

Outside Mexico City, however, monitoring and management of air quality fall largely under the jurisdiction of municipal governments that have neither the funding, the technical expertise, nor in some cases the interest in monitoring or managing air quality. Notable exceptions exist in Mexico's northern border region, where technical assistance and funding from the United States promoted the establishment of limited air quality monitoring networks in the binational cities in the early 1990s.

Mexico began establishing air quality monitoring networks in mid-sized cities throughout the 1990s, but only for a limited number of pollutants. (A detailed chronology is presented in table 7.8.) In 1989–1990, an emissions inventory study was conducted for the twin cities of Ciudad Juárez, Chihuahua, and El Paso, Texas, and an air quality monitoring system was established in Ciudad Juárez in 1993.[42] In 1993, after Sedesol trained a number of technicians, the Mexican government established a pilot program for vehicle inspections and maintenance in Tijuana. In 1992, Mexico initiated a study of fine particulate emissions for Mexicali, which shares an airshed with Imperial Valley, California.

These steps notwithstanding, in 1994, Mexico had permanent, automatic air quality monitoring networks in only four cities: Mexico

Table 7.8
Mexico's Urban Air Quality Monitoring Network

Year	City	Type of Monitoring
1980s	Mexico City	2 networks: 1 manual with 19 stations monitoring TSP, 5 monitoring PM10; 1 automatic network of 32 stations monitoring atmospheric conditions
1983	San Luis Potosí	Began with 7 stations monitoring SO^2 and TSP due to local iron and steel works
1993	Nacozari	Began with 4 stations monitoring SO^2 due to local iron and steel works
1993	Monterrey	5 stations (automatic) monitoring TSP, SO^2, CO, NO_x, VOCs; mobile monitoring also available
1993	Ciudad Júarez	Began with manual monitoring PM10, extended to automatic network in 1995 for CO and ozone.
1993	Cananea	5 stations in automatic network begun under La Paz agreement with United States:monitoring SO^2 in part from nearby iron and steel works
1994	Guadalajara	Automatic network of 8 stations monitoring TSP, SO^2, CO, NO_x, and VOCs
1994	Toluca Valley	Began with manual network in late 1980s, replaced in 1994 with automatic network of 7 stations monitoring TSP, SO^2, CO, NO_x, VOCs; mobile monitoring also available
1996	Querétaro	Began with 6 manual stations monitoring SO^2 and TSP
1996	Coatzacoalcos	Monitoring stations for ozone, NO^2, and CO operated by Pemex
1996	Tijuana	Began with 6 stations under Border XXI binational plan: 4 are automatic, monitoring NO^2, ozone, CO, SO^2; 2 stations are manual, monitoring PM10

(continued)

Table 7.8
(continued)

Year	City	Type of Monitoring
1997	Mexicali	6 stations under Border XXI binational plan: 4 are automatic, monitoring SO^2, NO^2, ozone, CO; 2 stations are manual, monitoring PM10
1997	Aguascalientes	1 automatic station monitoring NO^2, SO^2, and CO.
1996	Manzanillo	3 stations monitoring SO^2, NO^2, PST, and PM10
2000	Villahermosa, Tabasco	1 manual station
2000	Salamanca, Guanajuato	1 manual station
2000	Zacatecas, Zacatecas	1 manual station

Sources: Compiled by author from data available in INEGI, *México: Informe de la Situación General, 1999*; and Semarnap, *La Gestión Ambiental en México.*

City, Guadalajara, Monterrey, and Toluca (in the state of Mexico). In 1995, a similar network was established in Ciudad Juárez with the assistance of governments from the states of Texas and New Mexico, as well as the cities of El Paso, Texas, and Doña Ana, New Mexico. In 1997, two other northern border cities—Tijuana and Mexicali—began operating automatic, permanent networks, as did Manzanillo in the state of Colima. The network expanded significantly in 2000, with 7 additional cities starting up similar monitoring networks, for a total of 15 cities.[43]

By 1999, networks had been established in Guadalajara, Monterrey, Toluca Valley, Ciudad Juárez, Tijuana, and Mexicali.[44] Limited monitoring was done in Cananea, Querétaro, San Luis Potosi, Aguascalientes, Coatzacoalcos, Nacozari, and Manzanillo. The government also attempted to integrate federal, state, and municipal air quality control strategies through a series of management plans for major urban areas outside Mexico City. Between 1995 and 2000, the National Ecology Institute generated management plans, called *proaires*, for the cities of Mexico, Monterrey, Guadalajara, Toluca, Ciudad Juárez, Mexicali, and Tijuana.[45]

Several environmental standards promulgated by Semarnap during the Zedillo administration contribute to fuel switching and energy conservation in the power sector and within industries. These standards aim to reduce emissions, optimize combustion processes, and reduce fuel consumption. One of the most important of these is NOM-85, which sets stringent emissions standards for principal air pollutants, thereby driving fuel switching from coal and oil to natural gas. Another important standard is NOM-086, which addresses the environmental quality of fuels.

Striving for Sustainability

Air quality remains a problem in Mexico's urban areas, although the serious health threat to Mexico City's residents from worsening air pollution in the late 1980s and early 1990s has not been duplicated in other urban areas. Nationwide, ambient levels of lead and sulfur dioxide in the air appear to have dropped significantly from 1986 throughout the 1990s as a result of changes in vehicle fuels brought about by the Mexican government.

Air quality management is relatively recent in Mexico, and the impact of the government's current strategy in cities outside Mexico City is largely unknown. Environmentalists complain that the real state of air quality in many cities will not be known for many years, because ambient air quality in some large urban areas is monitored for only a limited number of pollutants and is not monitored continuously. Moreover the monitoring data are often unreliable because equipment is poorly maintained and operated.

The *Secretaría de Medio Ambiente y Recursos Naturales* (Semarnat) conceded that the monitoring networks for Mexico City, Monterrey, Guadalajara, Toluca, and Ciudad Juárez provide about 75 percent of the data that they are designed to provide. The remaining data are lost as a result of equipment breakdowns. According to Semarnat, however, data from the networks in Tijuana, Mexicali, Aguascalientes, Cananea, Coatzacoalcos, Manzanillo, Nacozari, Querétaro, and San Luis Potosí are less reliable.[46]

Obvious challenges remain. One World Bank study indicates that the Mexico City area still fails to meet Semarnat's standards for particulates 25 percent of the time, and for ozone 90 percent of the time.[47] According to Mexico's own pollution indexing system, Mexico City continues to suffer chronic air pollution at lower levels, and the situation does not appear to be improving.[48] However, in 2000, Semarnap reported that the annual average levels of particulates have been dropping steadily since 1997, carbon monoxide levels are significantly lower, and lead levels are negligible.[49]

Mexico City's 3.5 million vehicles are responsible for 84 percent of all emissions, and about 50 percent of these are from cars and buses built before 1990 and before catalytic converters were introduced into Mexico. Mexico is negotiating with automobile manufacturers to shorten the lag time—currently about six years—it takes for pollution control technologies to reach the Mexican market from other parts of North America. Semarnap officials also are focusing on the creation of new strategies aimed at implementing standards for vehicle emissions, vehicle inspection and maintenance programs, and new enforcement efforts aimed at stationary sources of air pollution. Officials have monitored vehicular emissions as part of pilot projects in several regions of Mexico.

For the rest of Mexico, the government has yet to implement a nationwide air emissions inventory of fixed sources of air pollution, and many industries still are not reporting their emissions to either local, regional, or federal government agencies. (See table 7.9.) The government has so few data on stationary industrial sources of air contaminants outside the Mexico City area that the country has been unable to participate fully in the trilateral pollution registry established by the North American Commission for Environmental Cooperation (CEC). The lack of data makes it difficult to implement air quality management programs.

In addition to insufficient data, Mexico maintains industrial air emissions standards that are lower than those in the United States.

Table 7.9
Change in Mexico's Monitoring of Industry, 1986–2000
(in percent)

Year	Industry Emissions Monitored
1986	›1%
1992	5%
2000	~10%

Sources: Compiled by the author from information available in Sedesol, "Protección del Medio Ambiente, Acciones"; Sedue, "Aspects of Mexico's Environmental Policy"; INEGI, *México: Informe de la Situación General, 1999*; and Giugale et al., eds., *Mexico: A Comprehensive Development Agenda*.

As Mexico continues to develop in its northern border region, these lower standards generate political clashes when local and state governments in the United States fail to meet their own air quality standards. This has been a particular problem in the power sector. As construction of power plants continues in Mexico's northern border regions, these lower standards can contribute to pollution in common airsheds, unless the Mexican government continues its current fuel-switching plan in favor of cleaner burning natural gas. As one example of the coming political struggle, two electricity-generating plants being built outside Mexicali, Mexico—10 miles from the California city of Calexico—have generated opposition from California environmentalists and the state's local government officials.[50]

California officials complain that, if built in the United States, the plants would be required to be fitted with the best available control technology and continuous emission monitors, which are not required in Mexico. Additionally, Mexico does not impose any limits on carbon monoxide emissions, which are tightly regulated under the U.S. Clean Air Act. Mexico's standards for nitrogen oxides are lower than U.S. limits, and Mexico does not require the power industry to report data on particulate emissions.

MUNICIPAL SOLID WASTE

The Challenge

Since the 1960s, intense urbanization has driven millions of Mexicans into towns and cities; and fast-growing municipalities have never been given the funding to provide adequate municipal services. One of the results has been tons of municipal waste that is never collected or is collected but tossed into open, unlined pits that ultimately contaminate underground water supplies.

In the 1980s, the federal government began working with municipal governments to ensure that garbage was collected rather than abandoned. A report by the *Secretaría de Desarrollo Urbano y Ecología* (Sedue) during the mid-1980s detailed the growing struggle with municipal waste in Mexico City. For the 1986–1987 fiscal year, Sedue set a modest goal of increasing the disposal of municipal waste in Mexico City from 40 percent to 60 percent of the waste generated. The secretariat expressed a willingness to obtain loans from multilateral institutions to implement a program that would allow the city to dispose of up to 80 percent of its waste.

For most of the 1990s, about 70 percent of municipal waste was collected; of that amount, more than 70 percent was badly managed. (Table 7.10 provides a breakdown.) By 1998, the percentage of garbage collected was significantly higher than it had been over the past two decades. That year, Semarnap estimated that 85 percent of municipal waste was collected but only about 60 percent of it was safely handled. Because poorly managed municipal waste is contributing to increasing groundwater contamination—an issue of substantial concern to the Fox administration—in early 2001, Semarnat officials said that better collection and handling of municipal waste must also be a priority.

Evolution of Waste Management

The Mexican government began making an effort to systematically reduce the amount of abandoned municipal waste in the mid-1980s. Pressures to address this problem came from Mexico City and from

Table 7.10
Mexico's Municipal Waste Management, 1992–1998

Year	Amount Generated (thousands of tons)	Percentage Collected	Percentage Badly Managed	Percentage Abandoned
1992	21,967.5	70	70	30
1993	28,089.5	70	75	30
1994	29,472.4	70	75	30
1995	30,509.6	70	73	30
1996	31,959.4	70	62	30
1997	29,272.4	77	55	23
1998	30,550.5	86	39	15

Sources: Compiled by author from data available in Sedue, "Aspects of Mexico's Environmental Policy"; Sedue, *Informe de Labores, 1986–1987 (1 de Septiembre de 1986 al 31 de Agosto de 1987)* (Mexico City, 1987); Sedue, Instituto Nacional de Ecología, *México: Informe de la Situación General, 1993–1994*; and INEGI, *México: Informe de la Situación General, 1999.*

the U.S.-Mexican border region, where rapid growth and urban deterioration were affecting both sides of the border.

Recognizing that many Mexican cities had no sanitary landfills, in 1994, the federal government promulgated a regulation establishing conditions under which sanitary landfills were to be built. The government also initiated a series of studies to characterize the pollution problems generated by the open-pit method of garbage disposal and presented a cleanup plan and one for construction of new disposal facilities in 50 cities.[51] Federal efforts aimed at improving the efficiency of municipal collection have yielded some benefits. In 1997, the percentage of garbage placed in municipal dumps began to increase, and throughout the decade, the number of disposal facilities has more than doubled.

Striving for Sustainability

World Bank estimates indicate that for Mexico to keep and increase water and sanitation coverage at reasonable service levels, the government will need to invest more than $1 billion per year for the next 10 years—more than three times the amount reportedly invested in 1998. With the decline in federal funds for infrastructure improvements, this financing would have to come from user fees, the private sector, and funds allocated to state and municipal governments—none of which immediately appears to be a viable source for the funding shortfall.

INDUSTRIAL AND TOXIC WASTE

The Challenge

The Mexican government has never implemented an effective, mandatory inventory of industrial wastes. As a result, government estimates of annual waste generation vary widely; therefore, the extent of the problem is not known. However, in some regions, such as states with substantial oil and production activity, the effects of this waste are evident. In Campeche, Quintana Roo, Tabasco, and the state of Mexico, some level of toxic chemicals has contaminated up to 40 percent of the land.

Although a nationwide waste inventory is not in place, the Mexican government has received some partial accounting of wastes and has estimated national totals from this partial accounting. In 1994, the 31 Mexican states and the Federal District of Mexico City reported 5.3 million tons of waste generated within their boundaries, and Semarnap estimated that these reports represented about 66 percent of the 7.7 million tons generated that year.[52]

Every few years, the estimates of waste generation change as the government refines its accounting and tracking procedures. Thus, in 1997, Semarnap estimated that the generation of hazardous waste in Mexico had grown from about 6 million tons of waste in 1990 to more than 12 million tons in 1997.[53] By 1998, however, Semarnap was estimating that about 3.2 million tons of hazardous waste were being generated, a statistic that was repeated in Semarnap's 1999 estimate of hazardous waste generation.[54] The World Bank estimated that 5.29 million tons of hazardous waste were generated in 1992, of which 3 million tons were abandoned.[55]

Although estimates of waste generation vary substantially, evidence suggests that little of the waste is handled or disposed of safely, because the number of Mexican facilities that can handle waste disposal has declined over the years as the amount of waste has risen. In 2001, only one hazardous waste disposal facility was in operation—near Monterrey in northern Mexico—and that facility held an estimated 550,000 tons of waste. Another facility in Hermosillo was closed in 1998, after local activists drew attention to inadequate management practices. Additionally, over the years, the Mexican government has identified hundreds of abandoned and health-threatening hazardous waste sites.

Mexico also lacks capacity in waste treatment as well as disposal. In 1996, only an estimated 12 percent of hazardous industrial waste generated in Mexico annually received proper treatment.[56] In 1997, Semarnap officials estimated that Mexico had the installed capacity to treat only about 26 percent of all hazardous waste and was not sure how much of that capacity was utilized.[57]

Evolution of Waste Management

Mexico had few controls over industrial chemicals until 1987, when the federal government published the first official manual for pesticide use and application,[58] and formed a commission to study the control of pesticides, fertilizers, and other agricultural chemicals. Mexico also began a registration program as well as a training program for agricultural producers.

One of the first times Mexico dealt with the issues of hazardous waste management and disposal was in the early 1980s, as foreign direct investment from the United States began to pour into Mexico's northern border states. Compared with heavy industries, the assembly plants did not produce substantial amounts of hazardous waste, but Mexico's ability to deal with industrial waste was very limited. In response, Mexico and the United States agreed to an annex to the 1983 U.S.-Mexico Agreement on Cooperation for the

Protection and Improvement of the Border Environment (the La Paz agreement), which required U.S. companies operating in Mexico's border region to export the chemical wastes they produced, including hazardous wastes, back to the United States.

However, because Mexico does not have reliable data on the total generation of hazardous waste, for many years the federal government was unable to enforce the provisions of the La Paz agreement that require the mostly U.S.-owned *maquiladora* industry to return wastes to the country of origin.[59] Compliance in reporting and tracking hazardous waste is improving under the new binational hazardous waste recording system called Haztraks (Hazardous Waste Tracking System). In 1991, only 200 out of 1,855 *maquiladoras* sent their hazardous waste back to the United States under the La Paz agreement. With Haztraks—which was implemented about the same time that the North American Free Trade Agreement (NAFTA) went into effect—by 1996 compliance rose to 86 percent for industries in the northern border region.[60]

The Mexican government established legal authority over waste generated by domestic industries in 1988, when a number of waste regulations were promulgated under the new omnibus environmental act. These initial regulations established principles for the installation and operation of hazardous waste facilities as well as principles governing the importation and exportation of wastes.

A 1989 study of the Mexico City area served as a basis for estimating the amount of hazardous waste produced nationwide. Industrial solvents represented the largest volume generated. In 1993, Mexico implemented a series of regulations defining various categories of hazardous wastes and their toxicity as well as a series of changes to environmental regulations designed to reduce air-based and water-based levels of lead. The hazardous waste regulations forced some large industries to improve their record keeping on wastes, although as late as 1999, the government conceded that it had little confidence in its own estimates of waste generation.[61]

By 1994, Sedesol officials had not implemented a hazardous waste inventory for Mexico, but the ministry did identify 265,427 industries capable of producing such wastes.[62] Almost all of these were micro-, small- and medium-sized businesses, and the government speculated that these businesses were not contributing wastes in volumes any higher than the total that had already been documented for large industries.[63] After a concerted record-keeping effort from 1989 through 1996, the federal government had a somewhat better profile of its waste generators—what they were producing and where it was stored.[64]

Mexican policy, like the policies of most industrialized countries, sets a priority on waste reduction and recycling rather than ultimate disposal. The amount of hazardous waste sent to authorized handlers increased steadily through the 1990s, although the percentage of total waste generated that these totals represent is not known. From about 20 such facilities in 1992, the number had grown to nearly 130 by 1997.[65] At various times, Sedesol and Semarnap have issued estimates of the amount of waste sent to authorized handlers, and these statistics indicate that the total rose from 70,000 tons in 1992, to 193,000 tons in 1994, and finally to 394,000 tons in 1997. In 1994, for example, Mexico had 12 firms that recycled solvents, 8 firms that recycled used acids, 9 firms that recycled metals, 4 firms that transported hazardous wastes, and 4 firms that collected and temporarily stored wastes. Another 10 firms recycled petroleum wastes primarily generated by Pemex, and 4 firms stored petroleum wastes. Two Mexican subsidiaries of multinational firms incinerated hazardous wastes.

The international community has had an influence on the Mexican government's philosophy of hazardous waste management. In addition to the U.S. influence on waste tracking along the northern border, Mexico also abides by the Basel Convention on Transboundary Movement of Hazardous Wastes and Their Disposal, which the government ratified in 1992. The Basel Convention recommends on-site treatment of wastes whenever possible or treatment as close to the source of generation as possible. When Mexico became a member of the OECD in 1994, the government agreed to implement other changes in its hazardous waste management policies. For example, in 1997, Mexico adopted a prohibition against exporting hazardous wastes to a non-OECD country, except for recycling purposes.

In 1995, as part of the CEC's work program to phase out certain persistent organic pollutants (POPs) within all three NAFTA countries, Mexico began a concerted effort to manage the production and use of other toxic chemicals. The program falls under a treaty on persistent organic pollutants finalized by 122 countries in December 2000. The terms of the treaty require governments to minimize and eliminate a number of toxic chemicals. Initially, control measures applied to a list of 12 chemicals: eight pesticides (aldrin, chlordane, DDT, dieldrin, endrin, heptachlor, mirex, and toxaphene); two industrial chemicals (polychlorinated biphenyls [PCBs] and hexachlorobenzene); and two by-products of industrial processes (dioxins and furans).

The NAFTA parties have developed action plans for managing the production and use of mercury, PCBs, DDT, and chlordane. The parties also determined that North America has no production or registered uses for many of the other pesticides detailed in treaty negotiations. The CEC is considering action on dioxins, furans, and hexachlorobenzene. Under cooperative efforts sponsored by the CEC, Mexico has agreed to phase out the use of PCBs, mercury, DDT, and chlordane. Mexico has also reduced the amount of DDT used by about 50 percent since 1997.[66] The three countries agreed to a 50 percent reduction in the use of mercury by 2006; the figure is based on emissions inventories conducted in 1990 or on an equivalent.

Striving for Sustainability

The gap between waste generation and waste handling and disposal remains large in Mexico, implying that many wastes are still abandoned. Mexico's only authorized hazardous waste disposal site holds 550,000 tons, but it is estimated that the country produces at least 3.2 million tons of hazardous waste per year, and possibly much more. Using the same logic, little of Mexico's waste appears to be safely handled: government figures from as late as 1997 show that only about 394,000 tons of hazardous waste were sent to authorized handlers.

To the extent that wastes are abandoned, they likely contribute substantially to the contamination of Mexico's dwindling water supplies. Wastes abandoned in open pits not only are an unknown health factor but also contribute to groundwater contamination that is almost irreversible. The extent of this problem is unknown, however, because Mexico's estimates of hazardous waste generation, handling, and disposal are based on incomplete and often faulty data.

Mexico has made great strides in the inventory, tracking, and export of hazardous wastes from U.S.-owned assembly plants in its northern border region. But by Mexico's own estimates, only 24 percent of hazardous waste is generated in this region.[67] The majority—65 percent—is generated in central Mexico, and this is where the focus of inventories and tracking of wastes should be.

Before Mexico can expand its pollution prevention programs, the federal government will need to implement consistent monitoring of industrial emissions and gather more information on individual facilities. Profepa's current Clean Industry audit program should assist in that effort, although at present the program does not extend to smaller industries.

Mexico's small industrial facilities are only lightly regulated, and the Economic Ministry collects most of the data on these facilities. Over many years, Mexican environmental officials have consistently said that the Economic Ministry refuses to provide environmental officials with much information on these smaller operations. Thus, in addition to regulatory changes, the Mexican government will need to establish a culture of interagency cooperation.

SUMMARY

Mexico faces substantial challenges in its efforts to reverse the unsustainable use of its water resources, to clean up water pollution, and to first halt and then reverse the related processes of deforestation and soil erosion. The costs of tackling these problems simultaneously are staggering, particularly given the uneven trend in Mexico's rate of economic growth, which periodically results in a decrease in the federal budget. Much of the existing contamination of surface and underground water must be addressed by construction of a very expensive urban infrastructure, which will require Mexican businesses and consumers to adopt a "pay as you go" approach to pollution.

Despite the current challenges of safeguarding water and land resources, the Mexican government's ability to manage urban air pollution, to track industrial chemicals, and to manage persistent organic pollutants has improved in recent years. The improvement appears to be partly attributable to technical assistance from other countries and multilateral institutions.

Notes

[1] Tim Weiner, "Mexico Grows Parched, With Pollution and Politics," *New York Times*, April 14, 2001, sec. A, p. 3.

[2] Instituto Nacional de Estadística, Geografía e Informática, *Estadísticas del Medio Ambiente, México: Informe de la Situación General en Materia de Equilibrio Ecológico y Protección al Ambiente,* vol. 2: *1999*, published in conjunction with Instituto Nacional de Ecología, Secretaría de Medio Ambiente, Recursos Naturales y Pesca (Mexico City, 2000).

[3] Richard Huber, Jack Ruitenbeek, and Ronald Serôa da Motta, *Market-Based Instruments for Environmental Policymaking in Latin America and the Caribbean: Lessons from Eleven Countries* (Washington, D.C.: World Bank, 1997), p. 65.

[4] Weiner, "Mexico Grows Parched," p. 3.

[5] World Bank, Country Operations I and Environment Division, Country Department II, Latin America and the Caribbean Region, "Staff Appraisal Report, Mexico Environmental Project," Report no. 10005-ME, Washington, D.C., March 9, 1992.

[6] Ibid.

[7] Instituto Nacional de Estadística, Geografía e Informática, *Estadísticas del Medio Ambiente, México: Informe de la Situación General en Materia de Equilibrio Ecológico y Protección al Ambiente,* vol. 1: *1997–1998,* published in conjunction with Instituto Nacional de Ecología, Secretaría de Medio Ambiente, Recursos Naturales y Pesca (Mexico City, 1999), p. 121.

[8] Huber et al., *Market-Based Instruments,* p. 65.

[9] Secretaría de Medio Ambiente, Recursos Naturales y Pesca, "Programa Nacional de Medio Ambiente, 1995–2000, Resume Ejecutivo," Mexico City, 1994.

[10] Environmental Secretary Victor Lichtinger, presentation for the Mexico Project, Americas Program, Center for Strategic and International Studies, Washington, D.C., May 18, 2001.

[11] U.S. Environmental Protection Agency, Office of Wastewater Management, "Water Pollution Control, 25 Years of Challenges for the New Millen-

nium," Publication no. USEPA 833-F-98-003, Washington, D.C., June 1998; also available at www.epa.gov (July 1, 2001).

[12] Secretaría de Desarrollo Social, Instituto Nacional de Ecología, *México: Informe de la Situación General en Materia de Equilibrio Ecológico y Protección al Ambiente, 1993–1994* (Mexico City, April 1994), p. 124.

[13] Elisabeth Malkin, "Mexico: Uphill Battle," Natural Resources Council Report, Summer 2000, Reuters Business Briefing, www.breifing.reuters.com (July 10, 2001).

[14] Organization for Economic Cooperation and Development, *Environmental Performance Reviews: Mexico* (Paris, 1998), p. 65.

[15] "CNA Blasts 'Nonpayment Culture'—Mexico," *Financial Times*, June 15, 2001, Business News Americas section; see also various National Water Commission databases found at www.semarnap.gob.mx (July 19, 2001).

[16] Marcelo M. Giugale, Olivier Lafourcade, and Vinh H. Nguyen, eds., *Mexico: A Comprehensive Development Agenda for the New Era* (Washington, D.C.: International Bank for Reconstruction and Development, World Bank, 2001), p. 624.

[17] Weiner, "Mexico Grows Parched."

[18] EPA, "Water Pollution Control."

[19] The figures in both tables are based on Mexican government data but are taken from databases from different periods.

[20] Secretaría de Medio Ambiente, Recursos Naturales y Pesca, *La Gestion Ambiental en México* (Mexico City, October 2000), p. 87.

[21] OECD, *Environmental Performance Reviews: Mexico*, pp. 109–110.

[22] Semarnap, *La Gestión Ambiental en México*, p. 87.

[23] OECD, *Environmental Performance Reviews, Mexico*, p. 192.

[24] INEGI, *México: Informe de la Situación General, 1999*, p. 85.

[25] Sedesol, *México: Informe de la Situación General, 1993–1994.*

[26] INEGI, *México: Informe de la Situación General, 1999*, p. 83.

[27] Victor Lichtinger, Presentation, May 18, 2001.

[28] OECD, *Environmental Performance Reviews: Mexico*, p. 98.

[29] Secretaría de Agricultura y Recursos Hidráulicos, Subsecretaría Forestal y de Fauna Silvestre, *Inventario Nacional Forestal Periódico, 1992–1994* (Mexico City, 1994), p. 21.

[30] Semarnap, *La Gestion Ambiental en México*, p. 89.

[31] World Bank, "Staff Appraisal Report, Mexico Environmental Project."

[32] Ministry of Urban Development and Ecology (Secretaría de Desarrollo Urbano y Ecología), "Mexico: Environmental Issues," Fact sheet, Washington, D.C., Embassy of Mexico, September 1992.

[33] Secretaría de Medio Ambiente, Recursos Naturales y Pesca, "Reforestación primeros saldos," *Desarrollo Sustentable* 2, no. 15 (July 2000): 16.

[34] Ministry of the Environment, Natural Resources and Fisheries (Secretaría de Medio Ambiente, Recursos Naturales y Pesca), *Mexico: Policies to Promote Sustainable Development* (Mexico City, April 2000).

[35] Semarnap, *La Gestion Ambiental en México*, p. 94.

[36] INEGI, *México: Informe de la Situación General, 1999*, p. 94.

[37] Secretaría de Medio Ambiente, Recursos Naturales y Pesca, Subsecretaría de Recursos Naturales, "Acciones de Conservación y Restauración de Suelos por Microcuencas," Mexico City, 1999.

[38] INEGI, *México: Informe se la Situación General, 1999*, p. 269.

[39] Semarnap, *La Gestión Ambiental en México.*

[40] Instituto Nacional de Estadística, Geografía, e Informática, "Avances en el Desarrollo de Indicadores para la Evaluación del Desempeño Ambiental en Mexico, 1997," published in conjunction with Secretaría de Medio Ambiente, Recursos Naturales y Pesca, Instituto Nacional de Ecología, Mexico City, September 1998, p. 37.

[41] Malkin, "Mexico: Uphill Battle."

[42] Sedesol, *México: Informe de la Situación General, 1993–1994.*

[43] Semarnap, *México: Policies to Promote Sustainable Development*, pp. 270–271.

[44] INEGI, *México: Informe de la Situación General, 1999*, p. 185.

[45] Semarnap, *La Gestión Ambiental en México*, p. 266.

[46]According to data from Semarnat's Sistema Nacional de Información Ambiental, available at www.semarnat.gob.mx (July 30, 2001).

[47]Giugale et al., eds., *Mexico: A Comprehensive Development Agenda*, p. 693.

[48] INEGI, *México: Informe de la Situación General, 1999*, p. 194.

[49] Secretaría de Medio Ambiente y Recursos Naturales, Gobierno del Estado de Mexico, Secretaría de Ecología, Gobierno del Distrito Federal, and Secretaría de Salud, *Programa para Mejorar la Calidad del Aire de la Zona Metropolitana del Valle de México, 2002–2010* (Mexico City, March 2002).

[50] Diane Lindquist, "New Baja Plants Will Take Toll on Air Quality," *San Diego Union-Tribune*, June 27, 2001, sec. A, p. 1.

[51] Sedesol, *México: Informe de la Situación General, 1993–1994*, p. 247.

[52] Ibid.

[53] INEGI, "Avances en el Desarrollo de Indicadores," p. 40.

[54] The lower figures for 1998 are found in INEGI, *México: Informe de la Situación General, 1997–1998*, p. 795. For 1999, see INEGI, Semarnap, and Instituto Nacional de Ecología, *Indicadores de Desarrollo Sustentable en México* (Mexico City, 2000), p. 174.

[55] World Bank, "Staff Appraisal Report, Mexico Environmental Project."

[56] OECD, *Environmental Performance Reviews: Mexico.*

[57] INEGI, "Avances en el Desarrollo de Indicadores," p. 42.

[58] Secretaría de Desarrollo Urbano y Ecología, *Informe de Labores, 1986–1987 (1 de Septiembre de 1986 al 31 de Agosto de 1987)* (Mexico City, 1987), p. 89.

[59] Alan D. Hecht, Patrick Whelan, and Sarah Sowell, "Sustainable Development in the U.S.-Mexico Border: Past Lessons, Present Efforts, Future Possibilities," Paper presented on behalf of the U.S. Environmental Protection Agency at the Border Institute Conference, Southwest Center for Environmental Research and Policy, San Diego, California, April 11, 2000; available at www.OIA-BILAT/MEXICO/BriefigDocs/BorderPaper_April-11-00.wpd (April 15, 2000).

[60] OECD, *Environmental Performance Reviews: Mexico*, p. 181.

[61] INEGI, *México: Informe de la Situación General, 1999.*

[62] Sedesol, *Informe de la Situación General, 1993–1994*, p. 251.

[63] Ibid., p. 529.

[64] Ibid.

[65] INEGI, "Avances en el Desarrollo de Indicadores," p. 45.

[66] North American Commission for Environmental Cooperation, "North American Agenda for Action, 2000–2002: A Three-Year Program Plan for the Commission for Environmental Cooperation," Montreal, February 2000, p. 98.

[67] Semarnap, *Mexico: Policies to Promote Sustainable Development*, p. 41.

CHAPTER EIGHT

FROM MEXICO TO THE AMERICAS

WITH TECHNICAL ASSISTANCE AND FUNDING FROM OTHER NATIONS and international institutions, throughout the 1990s, the Mexican government was able to substantially reinforce its environmental regulatory regime and develop a number of new programs and techniques to assist in defining, quantifying, and addressing the nation's environmental challenges. It is doubtful that Mexico would have been open to this influence in the absence of deepening regional and global economic ties that provided incentives for many types of social and political development.

Although the U.S. influence on Mexico's environmental policy is only one of several influences, the U.S. factor is important for several reasons. For many years, the governments of the United States and Mexico have been forced to integrate their development policies in order to address the needs of cities that straddle each side of their shared border. But U.S.-Mexican economic linkages are equally important to the development of Mexican environmental policy, because they generate synergies under which different forms of assistance have flowed into Mexico in greater volumes since the North American Free Trade Agreement (NAFTA) was signed. This support includes multilateral lending for environmental projects; environmental assistance from individual U.S. government agencies; and advice and assistance from international environmental groups, other nations, and other organizations.

As a result of both domestic and international influences, Mexico is gaining the environmental management expertise it needs to address the challenges posed by the state of the country's environment. With the implementation of geographical information systems, the expansion of environmental monitoring networks, and the reporting demands of multilateral institutions, the Mexican government has expanded its knowledge base about the state of its environment. The ability to measure the rates of resource depletion and to identify pollution sources and pathways will help the government in planning its remediation efforts.

Nevertheless, as the Mexican government gains competence in environmental management over time, the magnitude of the challenges the country faces is increasing substantially. In effect, a race has begun in which the Mexican government must move ever more quickly and forcefully to overcome larger environmental obstacles to continued economic development. The economic integration between Mexico and the United States under NAFTA can continue to benefit Mexico to the extent that the U.S. government is willing to offer—and the Mexican government is willing to accept and sustain—technical assistance that bolsters environmental capacity building.

NORTH VERSUS SOUTH: MERGING PRIORITIES

When Mexico agreed to an environmental agreement under NAFTA, immediate clashes resulted from differing environmental priorities among the three parties. These clashes reflected, in part, differing levels of institutional capacity to protect the environment. Similar clashes are likely to occur in setting an environmental agenda for the hemisphere. In general, Canadian and U.S. policy concerns merged on the following issues, and these were promoted in environmental negotiations:

- Countries should set their own environmental standards and be able to defend them against challenges posed by trade.
- Countries should enforce their own environmental standards so that no competitive advantage develops as result of lax enforcement of regulations.

- Compliance with environmental laws must be measured effectively.
- Foreign investment should be environmentally sound.
- Countries should work toward standardization of environmental monitoring and data collection so that like comparisons can be made across countries in deciding whether a nation is enforcing its environmental laws or whether shared resources are being depleted.
- Public participation is key to enforcement of environmental laws and establishment of sound, workable environmental management policies.
- Countries should work toward upward harmonization of environmental standards.

U.S. officials tried to institutionalize these common concerns within the environmental side agreement to NAFTA and through the activities of the North American Commission for Environmental Cooperation (CEC), the North American Development Bank (NADB), and the Border Environment Cooperation Commission. Efforts to carry out the U.S. agenda, however, often have been slowed by Mexico's need not only to mature its environmental institutions but also to develop a culture and tradition of environmental protectionism. Mexican institutions are faced with the following limitations:

- inability to make environmental management decisions based on sound science;
- inability to monitor industrial emissions, use of natural resources, and health of the ecoregion;
- industry's limited access to environmental technology;
- the government's lack of access to the capital needed to fund environmental programs and remediation efforts and to improve urban infrastructure;
- narrow scope of basic environmental standards;
- inexperience in conducting environmental assessments;

- lack of credibility on enforcement and compliance issues;
- narrow scope of environmental management programs;
- lack of environmental information made available to Canadian and U.S. government officials or to Mexican nongovernmental organizations; and
- lack of continuity of a stable professional cadre across presidential administrations and other government agencies.

Entering environmental agreements under NAFTA forced the Mexican government to deal with these management limitations more rapidly than it might otherwise have done. To set in motion a program of environmental protection that would please both domestic constituencies and international critics, Mexico has constantly revised and modernized the institutions that deal with the protection of natural resources and the environment, establishing management techniques and programs that are similar to those in the United States. These changes are important because they not only address rapidly escalating domestic environmental challenges but also serve to increase Mexico's capacity to deal with constantly increasing obligations under international environmental agreements.

The three environmental and infrastructure institutions created as part of NAFTA have allowed Mexico to phase in changes to its ability to protect natural resources and to monitor sources of pollution. But some U.S. and Canadian officials believe that small to medium-sized Mexican businesses have suffered some financial setbacks under NAFTA, and as a result, they resist the implementation of new environmental programs. One Canadian official predicted that this resistance would be duplicated throughout Latin America among industries that initially suffer from increased foreign competition.

Given the continuing expansion of joint environmental planning, Mexican environmental priorities have moved closer to those in the United States and Canada over time. The priorities have not merged, however, and sometimes mutual environmental goals result from very different motivating factors. For example, the U.S. and Canadian governments often push the Mexican government to gather and publicize emissions data so that all three countries can begin the process of standardizing their approaches to environmental protection and regulatory compliance. The Mexican government has never emphasized enforcement of its environmental laws but has begun to give priority to environmental data gathering and emissions monitoring for other reasons: the government's increasing concern over the deterioration of natural resources, which is limiting the country's development. As a result, Mexico has begun an extensive process of monitoring and analyzing data that help the government characterize the state of Mexico's environment and identify stresses on natural resources, the rate of loss of resources, and the future limitations to economic development posed by the loss of natural resources.

LATIN AMERICAN CHALLENGES

At the end of the Zedillo administration, environmental ministry officials applauded the CEC's efforts to enhance public participation, enforcement efforts, and Mexico's technical capacity to manage environmental programs. The ministry also approved CEC's attempt to forge a common environmental agenda for North America. Mexican officials predicted that other Latin American countries participating in a Free Trade Area of the Americas (FTAA) cooperative effort on the environment would find the CEC's public participation process and ability to enhance technical management capacity particularly useful.

As previous chapters have shown, Mexico's environmental priorities are the following:

- to reverse its rapid rate of deforestation;
- to move to sustainable water use practices, reduce water contamination, and increase the supply of potable water;
- to reduce the amount of abandoned solid waste or wastes that are badly managed;
- to extend wastewater collection and treatment systems;
- to increase the country's capacity to manage and dispose of hazardous wastes; and

- to slow down the loss of biodiversity.

In the view of Mexican government officials, many Latin American and Caribbean countries share these environmental priorities, and environmental ministry officials expressed their desire to take a leadership role in developing an environmental agenda for the hemisphere. Several Mexican officials called for a survey of the pressing issues throughout the region. Underscoring the view of Mexican officials, Enrique Leff, director of the United Nations Environment Program's Latin American and Caribbean Office, recently stated that Latin American countries share environmental challenges that reflect a lack of environmental infrastructure. Indicators of the failure to invest in infrastructure improvement include the following:

- *Water contamination:* On average, throughout Latin America only 2 percent of water is treated.
- *Solid waste:* On average, only about 40 percent is adequately handled.
- *Air pollution:* Throughout Latin America, one of the single largest factors is the pollution contributed by medium-sized industries.

One reflection of shared priorities is the agenda Mexico has developed for building the capacity of other Latin American environmental programs. At the end of the Zedillo administration, environmental ministry officials suggested the following priorities for its developing environmental relationship with Latin America:

- assisting in the strengthening of protected natural areas;
- assisting in establishing forest sinks to reduce greenhouse gases and promoting the importance of tropical rain forests in halting the advance of the effects of climate change;
- promoting planning activities to address the adverse effects of natural disasters and forest fires, with a special emphasis on addressing the causes of forest fires in Brazil and Colombia;
- helping devise economic incentives that promote the use of environmental services;

- assisting in establishing a system of environmental accounting in determining a country's gross domestic product; and
- enhancing Latin American governments' ability to identify quantifiable goals for environmental management programs, beginning with the establishment of an environmental information clearinghouse for Central America, modeled after the approach taken by the CEC for North American environmental information.

Throughout Latin America and the Caribbean region, nongovernmental organizations, along with the environmental ministers of these governments, have begun to identify priority areas of environmental concern in the hemisphere through a series of meetings and consultations that began fairly late in negotiations for a trade agreement. The environmental ministers from the Americas met shortly before the April 2001 Summit of the Americas and identified three environmental problems that exert the greatest pressure on all Latin American and Caribbean countries: (1) deforestation, (2) deterioration of the urban environment, and (3) increased vulnerability to natural events. Mexico shares all these concerns, but its particular emphasis is on deforestation and problems of urban infrastructure. The infrastructure problems, in turn, contribute to Mexico's growing water crisis.

While governments of the Americas share some common environmental problems, they also share some common methods of solving them. These governments have entered into 272 environmental and sustainable development accords and agreements that use trade-related measures to achieve their goals. A first step in forging environmental cooperation and sustainable development as part of the FTAA process, therefore, may well be to establish a policy-coordinating body that can determine a long-term environmental agenda for the Americas, taking into account shared priorities and existing commitments.

FUNDING

North American environmental officials who deal extensively with Latin American countries believe that, when the FTAA agreement is signed and implemented, it will set in motion changes in the flow of foreign direct investment to various countries that will not have the environmental infrastructure in place to absorb this investment in a sustainable way. This outcome would reflect the Mexican experience in terms of its economic integration with the United States. The Mexican government's priorities within the North American environmental agenda continue to be on the resources that NAFTA and other international institutions can allocate to improving urban infrastructure, giving Mexico technology transfers and advice on managing wastes and on the technical abilities needed to put into force effective environmental standards. Mexican officials firmly believe the rest of Latin America will share this priority.

If other Latin American and Caribbean countries follow Mexico's example, they will turn to international financing not only for urban infrastructure projects but also for capacity building projects that will help establish better use of natural resources. Officials of the two NAFTA institutions that provide assistance for infrastructure improvements—those that were established for the U.S.-Mexican border region—quickly determined the need for such assistance after they were formed in 1994; otherwise, local communities would have been unable to take advantage of their services. One Mexican environmental official serving at the end of the Zedillo administration concluded in a November 2001 interview: "What Latin America wants is help with environmental capacity building and concessional technical assistance in cases where environmental capacity is lacking."

Officials in the environmental ministry said that Latin American countries will be carefully watching Mexico's experience with the North American Development Bank and other international funding institutions to determine if a similar funding mechanism for infrastructure projects can be implemented in other parts of Latin America. The limitations to future development posed by Mexico's water crisis are one reason that the Fox administration has expressed an interest in expanding NADB's mandate and the geographical area it covers. Mexican officials believe they need a way to catch up in the development of urban, agricultural, and industrial infrastructure not only to protect the environment but also to maintain a competitive position that can attract the direct foreign investment that fuels economic growth. The NADB board of directors has responded by expanding the type of projects the bank will fund to include, among others, new types of water projects. However, the NADB's geographical reach remains limited to the border area.

Over the past decade, Mexico also has relied on the World Bank, the Inter-American Development Bank, the Global Environment Facility, and the Japanese and U.S. governments to help finance a variety of capacity building projects designed to increase Mexico's efficiency in infrastructure planning, urban air quality management, and biodiversity protection, in addition to reversing the process of deforestation. Officials expressed enthusiasm about funding mechanisms that provide Mexico with a base from which the government can pool international resources with some of its own resources and those from private industry in order to stretch the country's environmental capital. For example, environmental ministry officials praised the Japanese government's help in establishing the National Center of Environmental Investment, which provides funds for environmental laboratories and for programs that deal with the management of hazardous waste and air pollution.

CHAPTER NINE

POLICY RECOMMENDATIONS

The Mexican government's environmental programs evolved rapidly throughout the 1990s, but the pace of the country's environmental deterioration proceeded even more rapidly. Because the Mexican government has estimated the rate of this deterioration at 11 percent of the country's gross domestic product (GDP) annually, whereas the annual growth of GDP is less, the government faces a substantial need to invest in measures that protect the environment. The Fox administration recognized this need by devising a fiscal reform package that would raise revenue for environmental infrastructure projects by charging user fees for natural resources and incorporating other market-based instruments into environmental protection policies. These proposals were largely unacceptable to the Mexican Congress. However, given the short-term threat to continued economic development posed by Mexico's water crisis, it is critical for the Mexican Congress to quickly approve some version of fiscal reform that eliminates or reduces water subsidies and institutes new environmental taxes and fees.

In the meantime, the Mexican government can take some short-term measures to continue the progress made in improving environmental management. One measure, which the government is pursuing, is to continue the process of decentralizing authority to local governments by giving these governments more control over water management and providing incentives to promote local cost recovery for environmental services.

Other measures aimed at utilizing the polluter-pays principle more fully include the following:

- stepping up criminal enforcement activities and coordinating criminal and administrative enforcement authorities' efforts;
- giving the Federal Office of the Environmental Attorney General complete control over enforcement of water laws but also encouraging voluntary compliance through the Clean Industry environmental auditing program;
- raising administrative penalties to discourage violations of environmental laws; and
- increasing industry transparency to allow development of a national pollutant release and transfer registry.

ENVIRONMENTAL AGENDA FOR THE AMERICAS

The North American Commission for Environmental Cooperation (CEC) has shown that it can serve as a vehicle to analyze environmental linkages in North America, to forge a common agenda among diverse countries, and to enhance that agenda through CEC work programs and other activities. Given its track record in North America, the CEC—in consultation with the Organization of American States—could extend its activities to identify common environmental interests throughout the hemisphere and to make recommendations for creating a cooperative environmental mechanism under a Free Trade Area of the Americas (FTAA) agreement. One approach might be to have modules of environmental cooperation in individual regions of the Americas administered initially by the CEC and perhaps ultimately by a separate body.

Latin American and Caribbean countries already have implemented more than 200 environmental agreements that are in some way linked to trade. One initial step toward forming a hemispheric environmental agenda might include a review of these existing agreements to determine if these mechanisms can be linked or duplicated in other areas, for example, Canada's environmental agreements with Chile and Costa Rica that are part of bilateral trade agreements.

If a strong environmental component is negotiated as part of the FTAA plan, each Latin American and Caribbean country could develop national action plans aimed at implementing such provisions. These action plans could be loosely modeled on those that have been successful for individual issues in North America. For example, on sound chemical management, each country could establish an action plan for managing and reducing the use of mercury, chlordane, and DDT; those plans could be modeled on the CEC's action plans under its sound chemical management initiative.

The CEC itself often models its work program to conform to mandates established by the United Nations Environment Program or programs set up by other global or regional bodies. This work should be continued on a regional scale when an environmental agenda is established for the hemisphere.

THE ROLE OF CANADA AND THE UNITED STATES

Canada and the United States represent the two most industrially advanced and wealthiest economies in the Americas. They are the two countries with well-developed environmental capacity and a large public demand for environmental protection. For all these reasons, Canada and the United States should contribute substantially to technical assistance projects dealing with the environment to the maximum extent possible under an FTAA agreement. Canadian and U.S. assistance should be in the form of funding and technical expertise, and the two governments also should set an example by demonstrating real progress in implementing their own multilateral environmental obligations.

THE VIEW FROM MEXICO

An informal survey of Mexican environmental officials at the end of the Zedillo administration elicited some views on how to form an environmental agenda for Latin America. These views were shared by many, but not all, environmental officials, who expressed their opinions as individuals, not as representatives of their respective organizations. Respondents' recommendations included the following:

- An environmental agreement should not begin with the premise that coordinated environmental efforts should be structured exactly as they were under the North American Free Trade Agreement.
- In setting a hemispheric agenda, governments should deal with the impacts of pollution. In evaluating the environmental effects of trade policy, the parties should pay attention to the role of environmental standards and how they work in each country.
- Because Mexico is more likely to share common concerns with Latin America than with Canada or the United States, Mexico should promote alliances with other countries in the Americas.
- As economies grow under the trade agreement, governments should review the environmental impacts of that growth. In measuring environmental performance, however, the parties should balance performance analysis against the economic pressures imposed on an individual government.
- To ensure that pollution havens are not created, governments should attempt to increase environmental monitoring and data analysis in those sectors or geographical regions where trade or investment-led growth is very rapid. For example, an analysis can be undertaken on the effects of investment on specific states or municipalities.
- Governments should devise mechanisms to maximize public participation in environmental decisionmaking.

BIBLIOGRAPHY

Authers, John, and Sara Silver. "Trying Times as Mexicans Prepare for an Austere Budget: The Treasury Secretary's Tight Fiscal Policy is Upsetting the Governors." *Financial Times*, October 16, 2002, The Americas section, p. 6.

Bendesky, León, Barbara Bramble, and Stephen Own. *Four-Year Review of the North American Agreement on Environmental Cooperation: Report of the Independent Review Committee.* Montreal: North American Commission for Environmental Cooperation, June 1998.

Bureau of National Affairs, "U.S., Canada Agree to Set Emission Limits on Regional Sources to Curb Ozone Transport." *International Environment Reporter* 23, no. 5 (March 1, 2000).

Campbell, Tim, George Peterson, and Jose Brakarz. *Decentralization to Local Government in Latin American Countries: National Strategies and Local Response in Planning, Spending and Management.* Regional Sector Study of Decentralization in Latin American Countries. Final report. Washington, D.C.: World Bank, 1995.

Cevallos, Diego. "Environment-Mexico: The High Cost of Environmental Destruction." Inter Press Service, March 8, 2001, www.nexis.com (August 2, 2001).

"CNA Blasts 'Nonpayment Culture'—Mexico." *Financial Times*, June 15, 2001, Business News Americas section.

DePalma, Anthony. "States in Mexico Trying to Avoid Bankruptcy." *New York Times*, May 10, 1995.

"DF to Maintain Water Subsidy—Mexico." *Financial Times*, July 24, 2001, Business News Americas section.

The Economist. Intelligence Unit. "Country Commerce: Mexico." London, September 30, 2000; also available at www.nexis.com (October 15, 2002).

_____. "Regulatory/Market Alerts—Mexico." London, September 30, 2000; also available at www.nexis.com (October 15, 2002).

Gilbreath, Jan. *Planning the Border's Future: The Mexican-U.S. Integrated Border Environmental Plan.* Lyndon B. Johnson School of Public Affairs, U.S.-Mexican Policy Studies Program, Occasional Paper, no. 1. Austin: University of Texas at Austin, March 1992.

Giugale, Marcelo M., Olivier Lafourcade, and Vinh H. Nguyen, eds. *Mexico: A Comprehensive Development Agenda for the New Era.* Washington D.C.: International Bank for Reconstruction and Development, World Bank, April 2001.

Grupo de Reflexión (Gustavo Alanis, Rayo Angulo, Regina Barba, Gustavo Carvajal, Luis Manuel Guerra, Rodolfo Lacy, Leonardo Martinez, Olga Ojeda, Fernando Ortiz Monasterio, Tiohoga Ruge, Carlos Sandoval, Gabriel Sánchez Díaz, Juan Alvarez Barroso, Raúl Arriaga, Ignacio Cabrera, Martha Delgado, Blanca E. Jiménez, Victor Lichtinger, Victor Meza, José Antonio Ortega, Gabriel Quadri, Sergio Sanchez, Héctor Sepúlveda, Raul Tornel, and Victor Urquidi). "México: Hacia una Política Ambiental Eficaz para el Desarrollo Sustentable." Policy paper presented to five Mexican presidential candidates, Mexico City, April 2000.

Hecht, Alan D., Patrick Whelan, and Sarah Sowell. "Sustainable Development on the U.S.-Mexico Border: Past Lessons, Present Efforts, Future Possibilities." Paper presented on behalf of the U.S. Environmental Protection Agency at the Border Institute Conference, Southwest Center for Environmental Research and Policy, San Diego, California, April 11, 2000, www.OIA-BILAT/MEXICO/BriefingDocs/Border Paper_April-11-00.wpd (April 15, 2000).

Huber, Richard, Jack Ruitenbeek, and Ronaldo Serôa da Motta. *Market-Based Instruments for Environmental Policymaking in Latin America and the Caribbean: Lessons from Eleven Countries.* Washington, D.C.: World Bank, 1997.

Instituto Nacional de Estadística, Geografía e Informática (INEGI). "Avances en el Desarrollo de Indicadores para la Evaluación del Desempeño Ambiental en Mexico, 1997." Published in conjunction with Instituto Nacional de Ecología, Secretaría de Medio Ambiente, Recursos Naturales y Pesca, Mexico City, September 1998.

_____. *Estadísticas del Medio Ambiente, México: Informe de la Situación General en Materia de Equilibrio Ecológico y Protección al Ambiente.* Vol. 1, *1997–1998.* Published in conjunction with Instituto Nacional de Ecología, Secretaría de Medio Ambiente, Recursos Naturales y Pesca. Mexico City, 1999.

_____. *Estadísticas del Medio Ambiente, México: Informe de la Situación General en Materia de Equilibrio Ecológico y Protección al Ambiente.* Vol. 2, *1999.* Published in conjunction with Instituto Nacional de Ecología, Secretaría de Medio Ambiente, Recursos Naturales y Pesca, Mexico City, 2000.

_____. *Indicadores de Desarrollo Sustentable en México.* Published in conjunction with Instituto Nacional de Ecología, Secretaría de Medio Ambiente, Recursos Naturales y Pesca, Mexico City, 2000.

Johnson, Pierre, Enrique Leff, and David Runnals. "The FTAA and Hemispheric Integration: Building a Triple-Win Strategy for Trade and Sustainability in the Hemisphere." Statement presented to the Hemispheric Trade and Sustainability Symposium, Montreal, April 18, 2001.

Kiy, Richard, and John D. Wirth, eds. *Environmental Management on North America's Borders.* College Station: Texas A&M University Press, 1998.

Lexington Group. "Industrial Environmental Management in Mexico: Results of a Survey." Report of project sponsored by the Japanese government, the World Bank, and Mexico's National Ecology Institute, 1997.

"Ley Federal de Transparencia y Acceso a la Información Pública Gubernamental." *Diario Oficial de la Nación*, June 7, 2002, www.gobernacion.gob.mx (August 15, 2002).

Lichtinger, Victor. "Informe de Labores del Primer Semestre de Gobierno, Dic. 2000–Mayo 2001." Comunicación Social, Secretaría de Medio Ambiente y Recursos Naturales, Mexico City, June 2001, www.semarnat.gob.mx (June 17, 2001).

Lindquist, Diane. "New Baja Plants Will Take Toll on Air Quality." *San Diego Union-Tribune*, June 27, 2001, sec. A, p. 1.

Malkin, Elisabeth. "Mexico: Uphill Battle." Natural Resources Council Report, Summer 2000, Reuters Business Briefing, www.briefing.reuters.com (July 10, 2001).

Mandel-Cambell, Andrea. "World News: Latin America and the Caribbean." *Financial Times*, June 12, 2001, p. 9.

Molina, Mario J. "Proyecto para el Diseño de una Estrategía Integral de Gestión de la Calidad del Aire en el Valle de Mexico, 2001–2010." Presentation on behalf of the Massachusetts Institute of Technology, Integrated Program on Urban, Regional, and Global Contamination, Mexico City, November 6, 2000.

Mumme, Stephen P. "Cleaning the Air: Environmental Reform in Mexico." *Environment* 33, no. 10 (December 1991).

Mumme, Stephen P., C. Richard Bath, and Valerie J. Assetto. "Political Development and Environmental Policy in Mexico." *Latin American Research Review* 23, no. 1 (1988).

North American Commission for Environmental Cooperation. "Capacity Building on Sound Management of Chemicals in Mexico, 1996–1999." Montreal, 2000.

_____. "CEC Council Communiqué." Press release, Guadalajara, Mexico, June 29, 2001, www.cec.org (July 18, 2001).

_____. "Helping Industry Improve its Environmental Performance." *Trio* (newsletter), Fall 2000, p. 8.

_____. "North American Agenda for Action, 1999–2001: A Three-Year Program Plan for the Commission for Environmental Cooperation." Montreal, n.d.

_____. "North American Agenda for Action, 2000–2002: A Three-Year Program Plan for the Commission for Environmental Cooperation." Montreal, February 2000.

_____. "North American Cooperation for the Sound Management of Chemicals in Brief." Montreal, n.d.

_____. "The Power of Pollutant Information in the Hands of the Public." *Trio* (newsletter), Fall 2000, p. 7.

_____. "Priorities for Reinforcing Management Capacities in Mexico." Montreal, June 2001.
_____. "Reducing Mercury in the North American Environment." *Trio* (newsletter), Fall 2000, p. 6.
_____. "Report of the Executive Director, Commission for Environmental Cooperation, Regular Session of the CEC Council." Dallas, June 12–13, 2000.
_____. "The Sound Management of Chemicals Initiative under the North American Agreement on Environmental Cooperation: Regional Commitments and Action Plans." Montreal, June 1998.
_____. "Summary of Environmental Law in Mexico." www.cec.org (July 4, 2001).
_____. "Tracking Dioxins to the Arctic." *Trio* (newsletter), Fall 2000, p. 1.
North American Development Bank. "Expansion of NADB Sectors of Activity." Board of Directors Resolution 2000–10, November 16, 2000, San Antonio, Texas, www.nadb.org (June 13, 2001).
_____. "Joint Status Report." Published jointly with the Border Environment Cooperation Commission, San Antonio, Texas, March 31, 2001, www.nadb.org (June 13, 2001).
_____. "North American Development Bank Moves Forward to Expand its Activities within Current Provisions of Charter." Press release, San Antonio, Texas, November 27, 2000, www.nadb.org (June 13, 2001).
Organization for Economic Cooperation and Development. *Donor Support for Institutional Capacity Development in Environment: Lessons Learned.* Report of the Development Assistance Committee, Working Party on Aid Evaluation, Evaluation and Effectiveness Series, no. 3, Paris, 1999, www.oecd.org (December 15, 2000).
_____. *Environmental Performance Reviews: Mexico.* Paris, 1998.
Pérez, Miguel, and Fabián Muñoz. "Inicia Federalismo en Guanajuato: El 'Estado Piloto' para la Descentralización, Declara Zedillo, Revisarán Funciones de Secretarías de Estado en la Entidad." *Reforma*, July 1, 1995.
Secretaría de Agricultura y Recursos Hidráulicos, Subsecretaría Forestal y de Fauna Silvestre. *Inventario Nacional Forestal Periódico, 1992–1994.* Mexico City, 1994.

Secretaria de Desarrollo Social, Instituto Nacional de Ecología. *México: Informe de la Situación General en Materia de Equilibrio Ecológico y Protección al Ambiente, 1993–1994.* Mexico City, April 1994.

_____. "Protección del Medio Ambiente, Acciones." Mexico City, June 5, 1993.

Secretaría de Desarrollo Urbano y Ecología (Ministry of Urban Development and Ecology). "Aspects of Mexico's Environmental Policy and the Environmental Situation in Mexico." Mexico City, April 1991.

_____. "Ecología: Concertación de Voluntades." Mexico City, December 1987.

_____. *Informe de Labores 1986–1987 (1 de Septiembre de 1986 al 31 de Agosto de 1987).* Mexico City, 1987.

Secretaría de Medio Ambiente, Recursos Naturales y Pesca (Ministry for Environment, Natural Resources, and Fisheries). "La Cultura del Agua." *Desarrollo Sustentable* 2, no. 15 (July 2000).

_____. *La Gestion Ambiental en México.* Mexico City, October 2000.

_____. "Mexico: Environmental Issues." Fact sheet, Embassy of Mexico, Washington, D.C., September 1992.

_____. *Mexico: Policies to Promote Sustainable Development.* Mexico City, April 2000.

_____. "Programa Nacional de Medio Ambiente, 1995–2000, Resume Ejecutivo." Mexico City, 1994.

_____. "Reforestación primeros saldos." *Desarrollo Sustentable* 2, no. 15 (July 2000).

_____. Procuraduría Federal de Protección al Ambiente. *Informe Trianual, 1995–1997.* 2nd ed. Mexico City, 1998.

_____. Subsecretaría de Recursos Naturales. "Acciones de Conservación y Restauración de Suelos por Microcuencas." Mexico City, 1999.

_____. "Balance de la Superficie Forestal, 1950–1997." Cuadro II.5.1.3, www.semarnat.gob.mx (July 4, 2001).

Secretaría de Medio Ambiente y Recursos Naturales. Comunicación Social. "Enviará Victor Lichtinger Propuesta al Congreso de la Union Para que las Industrias Registren Sus Emisiones y Transferencias

Contaminantes." Press release 104, June 2001, www.semarnat.gob.mx (July 4, 2001).

Secretaría de Medio Ambiente y Recursos Naturales, Gobierno del Estado de Mexico, Secretaría de Ecología, Gobierno del Distrito Federal, and Secretaría de Salud. *Programa para Mejorar la Calidad del Aire de la Zona Metropolitana del Valle de México, 2002–2010.* Mexico City, March 2002.

Servicio Universal de Noticias. "Nueva Politica Ambiental." Mexico City, June 4, 2001, Reuters Business Briefing Archives, www.briefing.reuters.com (June 18, 2001).

United Nations Environment Program. "Governments Finalize Persistent Organic Pollutants Treaty." Press release, December 10, 2000, www.unep.org (February 11, 2001).

_____. Comisión Económica para América Latina y el Caribe. "Consolidar los Espacios del Desarrollo Sostentable." In *Equidad, Desarrollo y Ciudadanía,* 1999, pp. 279–300; www.unep.ch/etu/ (October 10, 2000).

_____. United Nations Conference on Trade and Development. "A Thematic Summary of the 1st Briefing Session for Geneva Missions." Capacity Building Task Force, Geneva, March 17, 2000, www.unep.ch/etu/ (October 10, 2000).

_____. United Nations Conference on Trade and Development. "A Thematic Summary of the 2nd Briefing Session for Geneva Missions." Capacity Building Task Force, Geneva, June 6, 2000, www.unep.ch/etu/ (October 10, 2000).

United Nations, Global Environment Facility. "Project Performance Report 2000." GEF Council Publication no. GEF/C-17/8, April 10, 2001, www.un.org (August 4, 2001).

United States Agency for International Development. "Country Strategy: U.S., Mexico." Internal agency document, Washington D.C., June 1998.

United States Department of the Interior. "Criteria and Guidelines for Evaluating Projects and U.S.-Mexico Border Activities." Report prepared for the Border Environment Cooperation Commission, Washington, D.C., April 1995.

____. "U.S. Fish and Wildlife Service Cooperative Programs with Mexico, 1992–1993." Washington, D.C., 1994.

_____. "U.S.-Mexico Cooperation on Natural Resources Management and Biodiversity Conservation Accomplishments under the Babbitt/Carabias Administrations." Fact sheet, Washington, D.C., September 7, 2000.

_____. Fish and Wildlife Service. "Sixty Years of Cooperation Between the United States and Mexico in Biodiversity Conservation (1936–1996)." Published jointly with the Secretaría de Medio Ambiente, Recursos Naturales y Pesca, Mexico City and Washington D.C., 1997.

United States Environmental Protection Agency. "United States–Mexico Border Environmental Indicators, 1997." Publication no. USEPA 909-R-98-001. Published jointly with the Secretaria de Medio Ambiente, Recursos Naturales, y Pesca, Mexico City and Washington, D.C., 1998.

_____. Office of Wastewater Management. "Water Pollution Control: 25 Years of Progress and Challenges for the New Millennium." Publication no. USEPA 833-F-98-003, Washington, D.C., June 1998, www.epa.gov (July 1, 2001).

United States International Trade Commission. *The Year in Trade 2000: Operation of the Trade Agreements Program.* 52nd Report, USITC Publication 3428. Washington, D.C., June 2001.

Weiner, Tim. "Mexico Grows Parched, With Pollution and Politics." *New York Times*, April 14, 2001, sec. A, p. 3.

_____. "On Tourism, Mexico Now Thinks Green." *New York Times*, August 31, 2001.

World Bank. "Mexico Country Brief," September 2000, www.worldbank.org (June 21, 2001).

_____. "World Bank Approves $606 Million to Support Fiscal Decentralization in Mexico." Press release no. 2000/143/LAC, December 15, 1999, www.worldbank.org or www.shcp.gov.mx/ieo/n_docs11.html (June 21, 2001).

_____. Country Operations I and Environment Division, Country Department II, Latin America and the Caribbean Region. "Staff

Appraisal Report, Mexico Environmental Project." Report no. 10005-ME, Washington, D.C., March 9, 1992.

_____. Country Operations I and Environment Division, Country Department II, Latin American and the Caribbean Regional Office, "Staff Appraisal Report, Mexico, Northern Border Environment Project." Report no. 12603-ME, Washington, D.C., May 16, 1994.

World Economic Forum. Global Leaders for Tomorrow Environment Task Force. "Pilot Environmental Sustainability Index." In collaboration with the Yale Center for Environmental Law and Policy, Yale University, and the Center for International Earth Science Information Network, Columbia University, Davos, Switzerland, 2000.

APPENDIX

RESEARCH INTERVIEWS

For this study, interviews were conducted from September 2000 through March 2001 with officials from the following institutions:

- Canadian Department of Foreign Affairs and International Trade
- Centro Mexicano de Derecho Ambiental
- Commission for Environmental Cooperation, Joint Public Advisory Committee
- Commission for Environmental Cooperation, Secretariat
- Economic Commission for Latin America and the Caribbean
- Environment Canada
- Instituto Tecnológico y de Estudios Superiores de Monterrey
- Office of the U.S. Trade Representative
- National Roundtable on the Environment and the Economy of Canada
- National Wildlife Federation
- Secretaría de Comercio y Fomento Industrial
- Secretaría del Medio Ambiente, Recursos Naturales y Pesca
- Sierra Club
- Texas Natural Resource Conservation Commission
- Transition Team, President Vicente Fox, Mexico
- Unión de Grupos Ambientalistas

- U.S. Agency for International Development
- U.S. Department of Agriculture
- U.S. Department of the Interior
- U.S. Department of State
- U.S. Environmental Protection Agency
- Universidad Nacional Autónomo de México
- World Wildlife Fund

INDEX

Page numbers followed by the letter t *refer to tables.*

ABOUT THE AUTHOR

JAN GILBREATH IS a senior associate at the Center for Strategic and International Studies (CSIS) and an environmental policy specialist on issues related to developing countries. She has authored numerous publications on environmental linkages between trade and economic development, on environmental capacity building, and on U.S.-Mexican binational environmental management programs. She is former executive director of the Global Public Policy Series of Reuters Foundation-Carnegie Endowment for International Peace, where she worked to identify trends in globalization affecting quality of life and economic well-being.

Her recent writings include "Generating Electricity and Pollution Disputes along the U.S.-Mexican Border," *Hemisphere Focus* (CSIS, forthcoming); "Economic Integration's Effects on Air Emissions in Mexico's Refining and Electricity Generating Sectors" (Office of the Chief Economist, Latin American and Caribbean Region, World Bank, Washington, D.C., 2002); and "Shifting Pollution Patterns in the Production of Refined Oil Products and Industrial Chemicals Under NAFTA" (doctoral dissertation, The University of Texas at Austin, 2002).

Gilbreath holds a doctorate in public policy from the Lyndon B. Johnson School of Public Affairs at the University of Texas at Austin and a master of arts from the Institute of Latin American Studies at the same university.